NEW DIRECTIONS FOR TEACHING AND LEARNING

Marilla D. Svinicki, *University of Texas at Austin*
EDITOR-IN-CHIEF

R. Eugene Rice, *American Association for Higher Education*
CONSULTING EDITOR

Problem-Based Learning in the Information Age

Dave S. Knowlton
Southern Illinois University Edwardsville

David C. Sharp
University of Southern Mississippi Gulf Coast

EDITORS

Number 95, Fall 2003

JOSSEY-BASS
San Francisco

PROBLEM-BASED LEARNING IN THE INFORMATION AGE
Dave S. Knowlton, David C. Sharp (eds.)
New Directions for Teaching and Learning, no. 95
Marilla D. Svinicki, Editor-in-Chief
R. Eugene Rice, Consulting Editor

Microfilm copies of issues and articles are available in 16mm and 35mm, as well as microfiche in 105mm, through University Microfilms Inc., 300 North Zeeb Road, Ann Arbor, Michigan 48106-1346.

ISBN 0-7879-7172-3   electronic ISSN 1536-0768

NEW DIRECTIONS FOR TEACHING AND LEARNING is part of The Jossey-Bass Higher and Adult Education Series and is published quarterly by Wiley Subscription Services, Inc., A Wiley Company, at Jossey-Bass, 989 Market Street, San Francisco, California 94103-1741. Periodicals postage paid at San Francisco, California, and at additional mailing offices. Postmaster: Send address changes to New Directions for Teaching and Learning, Jossey-Bass, 989 Market Street, San Francisco, California 94103-1741.

New Directions for Teaching and Learning is indexed in College Student Personnel Abstracts, Contents Pages in Education, and Current Index to Journals in Education (ERIC).

SUBSCRIPTIONS cost $70 for individuals and $145 for institutions, agencies, and libraries. Prices subject to change.

EDITORIAL CORRESPONDENCE should be sent to the editor-in-chief, Marilla D. Svinicki, The Center for Teaching Effectiveness, University of Texas at Austin, Main Building 2200, Austin, TX 78712-1111.

Cover photograph by Richard Blair/Color & Light © 1990.

www.josseybass.com

CONTENTS

About This Series. Since 1980, *New Directions for Teaching and Learning* (NDTL) has brought a unique blend of theory, research, and practice to leaders in postsecondary education. We strive for not only solid substance but also timeliness, compactness, and accessibility.

This series has the following goals: to inform about current and future directions in teaching and learning in postsecondary education, to illuminate the context that shapes those new directions, to illustrate new directions through examples from real settings, and to propose how new directions can be incorporated into still other settings.

This publication reflects the view that teaching deserves respect as a high form of scholarship. We believe that significant scholarship is done by not only the researcher who reports results of empirical investigations but also the practitioner who shares with others disciplined reflections about teaching. Contributors to *NDTL* approach questions of teaching and learning as seriously as they approach substantive questions in their own disciplines, dealing not only with pedagogical issues but also with the intellectual and social context out of which those issues arise. Authors deal with theory, research, and practice, and they translate from research and theory to practice and back again.

About This Volume. Problem-based learning (PBL) is becoming a widely used instructional method because it addresses some of the key learning outcomes that we hope to achieve in higher education. This issue gives a thorough look at PBL—its history, theories, and practical implementation concerns. It also gives us a chance to look at a teaching method that has matured through use and study, rather than raw new methods still in the testing phases, a luxury we don't often have.

Marilla D. Svinicki
Editor-in-Chief

MARILLA D. SVINICKI is director of the Center for Teaching Effectiveness at the University of Texas at Austin.

EDITORS' NOTES

Problem-based learning (PBL) is a pedagogy that allows students to become actively engaged in their own educational processes. Furthermore, PBL allows professors to serve as guides and facilitators to students. Within these ideals of students' active engagement and professors' guiding and facilitating, students usually retain enough freedom to pursue their own rational self-interest by establishing personal goals related to problems and working to find viable solutions to those problems. As presented in this volume, PBL is framed by an understanding of the role of educational processes in the Information Age. When viewed with this frame, a volume about the design and implementation of PBL is useful for professors in all disciplines.

Theoretical Frame for This Volume

The last few words in this volume's title—"for the Information Age"—may seem initially to be an attempt by us to add buzzwords that will attract enlightened readers' attention to this volume. A cursory reading of this volume may seem to confirm the nonsubstantive inclusion of an Information Age slant. After all, only Chapter One of this volume makes any connection between PBL and the Information Age. And in fact, Chapter Six confirms that an imperfect design of PBL will not send higher education back to the Stone Age. But a reconsideration of the Information Age in terms of both the nature of knowledge and day-to-day problems will lead to the conclusion that PBL is a useful—and, indeed, necessary—pedagogical approach.

Information Age Knowledge. The defining characteristic of the Information Age is the availability of information. Therefore, knowledge must constitute more than simply accessing information. Information becomes knowledge only after processes of collaborative knowledge construction among students. That is, knowing only facts and figures is no longer substantive; interpreting information and disseminating those interpretations are more indicative of Information Age knowledge.

In the Information Age, such interpretations can vary widely. Thus, an important frame for this issue is that knowledge can be reconstituted from factual truths to individual and small-group interpretations. As evident in articles in this volume, one correct solution is rarely needed as a solution to a problem (see, for example, Chapters Seven and Eleven). Rather, professors can design environments (for example, Chapters Four and Five) in which students can arrive at numerous solutions, all of which may sufficiently address the problems at hand (for example, Chapters Six, Seven, Nine, and Ten). These solutions can be assessed more in light of their appropriateness for a specific situation than for their denotative accuracy (see Chapter Eleven).

Information Age Problems. Perhaps less theoretically obtuse is a second aspect to the frame of Information Age as a part of this volume. Whereas problems have always been pervasive in most walks of life, the conveniences of the Information Age have heightened and broadened the scope of problems that people routinely encounter. For example, as the technologies of travel have become more time efficient and free trade agreements have opened possibilities for international business relationships, corporate decision makers have more opportunities to expand operations and maximize profit. But opportunities of the Information Age are not always advisable, and decision makers must analyze and solve problems to implement substantive business relationships that are both profitable and ethical.

Similarly, the Internet and other information technologies have made information easier to access, but this ease has complicated the process of distinguishing between credible information high in value and propaganda riddled with inaccuracies. Sorting the "wheat" from the "chaff" of information requires consumers of ideas to make decisions about credibility and relevance of various sources. Even some types of expertise have become a thing of the past in the Information Age. "E-trading," for example, has allowed anyone with a computer to become a stock broker. As a result, though, solving problems related to understanding stock-market volatility have become commonplace.

Purpose of This Volume

Part of the educational process requires professors to help students acquire problem-solving skills so that they can help create and solve Information Age problems. But the task of helping students acquire problem-solving skills, in itself, presents problems to professors. As professors design and implement problem-solving activities, they will have to solve problems related to time constraints or limited resources. As professors implement PBL, they will have to solve interpersonal problems of resituating themselves in the classroom as a facilitator of learning, not simply a source of knowledge. These interpersonal problems will require professors to shift their thinking and view students as more than receptacles for content. Instead, in PBL, students are creators of knowledge.

Similarly, professors will have to consider philosophical questions regarding the nature of knowledge and the appropriateness of assessing students against an implied standard of objective and universal truth that students may not share. Said differently, with the decision to use PBL in the classroom, professors will encounter problems of their own that are related to the design and implementation of PBL. Not unlike PBL assignments to their students, the issues and obstacles professors will encounter require practical solutions as well. This volume can help professors solve such problems.

Overview of the Chapters in This Volume

This volume of *New Directions for Teaching and Learning* provides information about the theory supporting the need for PBL. It also offers articles that deal with the design and facilitation of PBL.

Philosophical and Theoretical Issues. The first two chapters deal with a theoretical consideration of PBL. In Chapter One, Dave S. Knowlton argues that problem solving is an essential component of a formal education, and without a problem-solving approach, professors are ignoring their responsibilities to educate students. In Chapter Two, Woei Hung, Jessica H. Bailey, and David H. Jonassen offer a theoretical perspective of PBL. Specifically, they examine numerous tensions that some professors may experience as they consider the ramifications of implementing PBL. These tensions—and their resolutions—are discussed in light of empirical literature regarding PBL's efficacy.

Design. Chapters Three and Four deal with the design of PBL. In Chapter Three, Renée E. Weiss focuses on the design of problems that will elicit higher-order thinking from students. The author describes numerous characteristics of "good problems." In Chapter Four, Deborah L. Lowther and Gary R. Morrison offer a model for integrating computers into the design of PBL activities.

Integration of Design and Implementation. Chapters Five and Six provide a transition from considering design to considering the implementation of PBL. In Chapter Five, Wayne A. Nelson describes how he used the concept of a "design studio" to transform traditional courses into project-based problem-solving environments. In Chapter Six, David C. Sharp describes how he implemented PBL into a Master's of Business Administration course. As part of the discussion of implementation, the author describes the process of designing the problem itself and the assignment guidelines that frame the problem.

Implementation and Facilitation. Chapters Seven through Eleven deal with implementing and facilitating PBL. Charles F. Abel's ideas in Chapter Seven culminate in a model based in heuristic thinking. His use of heuristics may be useful to professors across disciplines as they guide students through problem-solving activities. Collaboration is one characteristic of many PBL activities, and in Chapter Eight, Bruce W. Speck offers insights into forming collaborative groups and helping those groups work together effectively. In Chapter Nine, Julia Beckett and Nancy K. Grant offer strategies that professors can use as they facilitate problem solving among students who are engaged in field experiences. In Chapter Ten, Douglas J. Hacker and John Dunlosky suggest that professors not only must provide opportunities for students to solve problems but also must help students become aware of the *whys* and *hows* of their problem-solving approach. To this end, they provide a method for helping students approach their problem-solving activities metacognitively. Finally, in Chapter Eleven,

Rebecca S. Anderson and Jane B. Puckett address assessment of students' efforts in solving problems. Specifically, they provide insights into how professors can design rubrics that will serve as a basis for assessing students' work. In discussing how to use these rubrics, Anderson and Puckett suggest the need for students to assess not only their own work but also each other's work.

Conclusion

PBL may be a useful approach for bringing formal education in line with the Information Age. This volume can serve as an important resource for professors who are using PBL in the classroom. The articles in this volume span a broad range of issues associated with this method, and we hope that this volume will guide professors toward solving the problems they face as they design, implement, facilitate, and evaluate students within problem-based frameworks.

Dave S. Knowlton
David C. Sharp
Editors

DAVE S. KNOWLTON is assistant professor of instructional technology in the department of educational leadership at Southern Illinois University Edwardsville.

DAVID C. SHARP is assistant professor of economics in the division of business and economic development at the University of Southern Mississippi Gulf Coast.

1

The author argues that professors must engage students in problem-solving activities across all disciplines. To ignore students' problem-solving skills is to undermine the possibility of creating "educated individuals" through higher education.

Preparing Students for Educated Living: Virtues of Problem-Based Learning Across the Higher Education Curriculum

Dave S. Knowlton

This volume provides insight into many virtues of problem-based learning (PBL). In this article, though, I offer a broader and more philosophical argument for incorporating PBL into higher education. I begin by defining PBL and discussing how its characteristics are educationally useful. Then I develop and defend the argument that the academy as a whole cannot meet its mission of educating students unless students are engaged in problem-solving activities. In the final section of this article, I address some common objections to my argument.

PBL: Definitions and Virtues

Problems have two characteristics. First, a problem is an unknown, and second, value must exist in solving the unknown (Jonassen, 2000). *PBL,* then, is any pedagogical approach that requires students to solve for an unknown. Although such a definition may seem simplistic, Jonassen notes that not all problems are equivalent, and thus problem solving is not a rote activity. Therefore, PBL can take on many forms of both processes and products.

One common form of PBL is the "classic version" (Hmelo and Evensen, 2000) which is characterized by free inquiry among students and student-centered learning. Also, the classic version requires students to collaborate, formulate learning issues by determining factors that may contribute to the cause or solution of a problem, identify relevant content, and generate hypotheses. Most PBL models also contain student reflection components as a means of self-evaluation.

Inherent to both this classic version and other variations of PBL are numerous characteristics that are educationally principled. For example, inherent to PBL is a connection to self-directed learning; indeed, the connection between PBL and self-directed learning is well documented (see, for example, Williams, 2001; Hmelo and Evensen, 2000; Hmelo and Lin, 2000). As Blumberg (2000) notes, PBL and self-directed learning are not synonymous, but self-directed learning can result from PBL. Blumberg's position has been confirmed empirically. Participants in one study noted that engagement in PBL advanced their sense of being self-directed learners (Kaufman and Mann, 1996).

Beyond self-directed learning, PBL requires students to be active. Students who are actively engaged in the educational process make substantive connections with course content. These connections promote a deep level of processing. For example, requiring students to generate ideas and provide explanations to support those ideas promotes learning (Dominowski, 1998).

Another characteristic of PBL that is likely to promote learning is collaboration. Students often understand course material better when they interact with and learn from each other (Daiute and Dalton, 1993). Through collaborative learning and social interaction, students can help shape each other's ideas by providing feedback to each other. As students receive feedback, they can refine their ideas in light of that feedback and submit their newly shaped and refined thoughts to classmates for further debate and discussion.

Problem Solving and Purposes of Education

So far in this article, I have defined PBL and described how its specific characteristics can promote an active and collaborative environment. This type of environment is more likely to promote learning than a traditional classroom, which often only requires students to passively absorb and regurgitate information as organized and delivered by the professor. In the remainder of this article, I establish and defend a larger argument about the virtues of PBL. Namely, students cannot meet the basic criteria of "an educated person" unless they are adept at managing and solving problems. From this statement emerges an allied mandate to faculty members in higher education: Professors must engage students in PBL because to ignore problem-solving skills is to undermine the academy's responsibility to develop educated individuals.

I build this argument by noting a connection between the purposes of education and problem solving. Specifically, a formal education should prepare students for participation in the workplace, educate students in the liberal arts tradition, and help students learn about themselves.

Occupational Preparedness. Certainly, a formal education should prepare students for participation in the labor market. In the Industrial Age, successful employees often needed only rudimentary skills for understanding and following directions. Knowledge and information were finite; thus, procedures were relatively static.

In the Information Age, however, much of the content of business is shaped by social factors that constantly change (Zorn, 2002). As Goldsmith (2001) notes, "No longer can [organizations] depend on the same old answers, because [they] are faced with new problems" (p. 78). Because these socially constructed problems are systemic to business and industry, successful employees will be able to "serve in a strategic decision-making context. . . . [,] implement detailed operational plans and work toward strategic goals" (Whiteley, 1993, p. 2). The message from Zorn (2002), Goldsmith (2001), and Whiteley (1993) is clear: In the Information Age, an employee can contribute to an organization's success only by engaging in problem-solving activities. The importance of problem solving seems to be confirmed by Edney (1991), who notes that managers list employees' "rote" and "mechanical" approaches to problem solving as a chief concern.

Undeniably, as the dawn of the Information Age becomes a metaphorical midday, the nature of the workplace and the requirements of employees have changed. Therefore, the process of preparing students for the labor market necessarily must change. Said differently, learning in the real world is different from learning in classrooms (Jonassen, 2002). Traditional modes of classroom learning—often characterized by memorizing information and mirroring the views of professors—do not prepare students for the type of learning they will encounter in the real world. Learning in the real world is a product of problem solving. Such problem solving does not occur through processes of memorizing and mirroring; rather, it comes through processes of carefully defining and analyzing problems that exist in the organization for which one works.

Internships can bridge the gap between classroom learning and solving problems within organizations. But many students never hold internships or participate in field experiences. Therefore, professors have a responsibility to integrate into their classrooms the types of problems that students will encounter in the workplace.

Liberal Arts Education. Holmes (1996) notes that learning in the liberal arts tradition "takes the long-range view" of education by focusing on content and processes that prepare students to be "persons." Pedagogically, writing is at the heart of learning in the liberal arts tradition (Hersh, 1997), and writing is inherently a problem-solving activity (Lindemann, 1995). In one sense, then, problem solving is the heart of liberal arts. Professors who are teaching in institutions that support a liberal arts mission are bypassing that mission if they do not design their pedagogical approach to support problem-solving activities.

Beyond pedagogy, though, the definition of *liberal arts learning* as preparing students to become persons begs a question: What counts as valid content—not to mention valid knowledge that will come from studying the content—that can prepare students to become persons? Valid content and viable knowledge are often unknowns, and a liberal arts education depends on students solving for the unknown. It may seem to be overly dramatic to claim that curriculum and content themselves are the source of a problem that students must solve, but consider the difficulties of determining valid content in postmodern academia. Lang (1999) points to the difficulties by simply noting that "contemporary liberal arts curricula are . . . [often] substantially consumed by internal academic agendas" (p. 135). Less cynically, the postmodern academy perhaps has become more tolerant of what "great works" are worthy of inclusion in a liberal arts curriculum. In many disciplines, notions of a canonical literature or an essential set of content are obsolete, and professors who promote such essentialism are considered retrograde. Replacing the traditional ideas of a cannon and essential content is a dependence on the decisions of professors. Individual professors decide the scope of worthy content, and professors choose content for a variety of reasons, not all of which are based on principles of educational soundness or student need. For example, professors sometimes base their courses on content with which they are already familiar.

I am not lamenting the rise of postmodernism, the demise of essentialism, or the purview of professors to determine worthy course content. I am merely noting that the shifting paradigm sometimes leaves students in a quandary. They are left purposelessly to roam the academic landscape looking for the content that they, as individuals, need to become persons—that is, to become educated in the liberal arts sense. For each student, recognizing valid content and viable knowledge is in itself an act of problem solving. Professors, then, must support students' problem-solving efforts if a liberal arts education is to be important and viable.

Learning About the Self. Learning about the self is a corollary to both occupational preparedness and liberal arts learning. For example, career preparation is not just learning the content and processes of a career; career preparation also involves developing an understanding of how a career will fulfill—or fail to fulfill—students as individuals. Similarly, learning in the liberal arts tradition requires more than studying the content. As Holmes (1996) notes, the central question of liberal arts focuses on the individual: "What will all this stuff do to me?" (p. 24). Despite the overlap between this and other purposes of education, learning about the self deserves separate treatment as a purpose of education. In fact, some empirical evidence supports the connection between learning about the self and PBL (for example, Evensen, Salisbury-Glennon, and Glenn, 2001).

Specifically, the characteristics of PBL provide a unique opportunity for students to learn about themselves. As part of the problem-solving process, for example, students must consider their own educational goals (Bridges and Hallinger, 1997). In the context of some problems, determining educational goals is likely to require introspection about students' values, ethics, and beliefs. These types of problems may even highlight for students key differences among their beliefs, decisions, and behaviors. PBL activities provide an impetus for students to reconcile these differences, and in the process of reconciling them, students may learn more about themselves than they would learn in a traditional curriculum that simply focuses on the coverage of content.

Social interaction is another characteristic of PBL that provides the opportunity for students to learn about themselves. Hmelo and Evensen (2000) seem to support this perspective. They note that learners in a PBL environment can be seen both as "transforming" and "transformed." By examining how these transformations happen in the context of a PBL social system, students can gain insights about the ways they relate to, and are influenced by, other students. For example, through social interaction, students might discover their own propensity to stay silent even when they disagree with other members of the group.

PBL also provides students with opportunities to gain insights into their own approach to solving problems (Allen, Duch, and Groh, 1996). As students transition from solving problems (a cognitive activity) to learning about their own approach to solving problems (a metacognitive activity), they begin asking themselves numerous questions that will provide insights into who they are as learners: Which problem-solving strategies work well for me? Which ones do not? Why do some work well for me, but others do not? (For a fuller discussion of metacognition, see Chapter Ten.)

I am not suggesting that learning about the self is an automatic by-product of problem solving. Professors may need to act as facilitators so that students see how their engagement in problem-solving activities can teach them about themselves. Elsewhere in this volume (Chapter Eight) is a discussion of how professors can help facilitate students' understanding of group dynamics, which may help students consider their own role within a group. Instructional strategies—like journal keeping and role playing—can help students learn about themselves within PBL environments (Chapter Nine). Speck (1997) provides insights into helping students consider ethical dilemmas that they may face. All of these resources can help professors guide students toward learning about themselves in PBL.

Objections to the Virtues of PBL

As I have argued, if education is to meet its central purposes of occupational preparedness, liberal arts learning, and learning about the self, then PBL is indispensable. As I conduct faculty development workshops that establish and defend arguments similar to the ones that I promote in this article, I occasionally hear objections from administrators, professors, and even students. Hung, Bailey, and Jonassen in the next chapter of this volume address many tensions surrounding PBL, but in the remainder of this article, I address some additional common objections.

General Education Curriculum Should Emphasize Problem Solving. Many professors agree that problem solving is a worthy pursuit, but they suggest that PBL is more suited for the general education curriculum. In other words, they contend that general education courses should promote problem-solving abilities among students but that courses within a major—and certainly junior, senior, and graduate-level courses—should focus on content.

Numerous problems with this argument exist. Most basically, the scope of the general education curriculum is not broad enough to help students become adept at solving problems. Many universities do offer courses designed to introduce students to general learning skills, like problem solving. But it is naïve to assume that one semester (or even four) is an adequate "magic bullet" for helping students learn how to solve problems and gain fluency in problem-solving processes.

Furthermore, we must acknowledge that problem solving is domain specific. That is, solving problems in science is not the same as solving problems in the fine arts. Solving problems in mathematics requires a different approach from solving problems related to the study of literature. So, although many general education courses, like English composition, may emphasize problem-solving skills, these courses do not provide students with an adequate background for solving problems within specific disciplines.

Foundational Knowledge Must Be a Precursor to Problem Solving. Other professors and administrators assert that students are not capable of solving problems without a foundational knowledge of the discipline to support their problem-solving efforts. This is a valid argument to a point, but how much foundational knowledge is enough? Is it necessary (or even possible) for students to have *all* of the foundational knowledge associated with a discipline before they can tackle any problem? More provocatively, what do we mean by "foundational knowledge"? Typically, when faculty members point to a need for students to have a foundational knowledge, they really are advocating that students memorize information as a precursor to applying the information through problem solving. Rarely, though, does memorizing a database of knowledge assist students in solving problems.

PBL Is a Scam for Poor Teaching. Some professors and administrators have suggested that PBL reinforces habits of poor teaching. That is, the view persists that professors assign problems to be solved in lieu of lecturing and engaging students in more organized and directed teaching activities. In short, the skeptic argues that PBL allows professors to set their teaching responsibilities aside so they can focus on research while students solve problems without the guidance of a faculty member.

Admittedly, a fine line exists between student-centered approaches, like PBL, and bad teaching. I can point to examples of professors who confuse student centeredness with abdicating their responsibilities to students, and you probably can, too. What the various articles in this volume should suggest, though, is that executing PBL well takes more time on the part of professors, not less. Professors' responsibilities are not abdicated, only recast. Professors transition from playing solely an active role to playing both an active and reactive role in the teaching and learning process.

Conclusion

The opportunities for implementing PBL into the higher education curriculum are endless, and professors would do well to seize those opportunities. Problem-solving skills are a defining characteristic of an educated individual, and without a focus on problem solving, professors are ignoring their responsibilities to help students journey toward the educated life. When designed and implemented well, PBL can serve as a "road map" for professors who are guiding students on their journey and as a pathway and bridge for students who are traveling toward becoming educated individuals.

References

Allen, D. E., Duch, B. J., and Groh, S. E. "The Power of Problem-Based Learning in Teaching Introductory Science Courses." In L. Wilkerson and W. H. Gijselaers (eds.), *Bringing Problem-Based Learning to Higher Education: Theory and Practice.* San Francisco: Jossey-Bass, 1996.

Blumberg, B. "Evaluating the Evidence That Problem-Based Learners are Self-Directed Learners: A Review of the Literature." In D. H. Evensen and C. E. Hmelo (eds.), *Problem-Based Learning: A Research Perspective on Learning Interactions.* Mahwah, N.J.: Erlbaum, 2000, 199–226.

Bridges, E. M., and Hallinger, P. "Using Problem-Based Learning to Prepare Educational Leaders." *Peabody Journal of Education,* 1997, 72(2), 131–146.

Daiute, C., and Dalton, B. "Collaboration Between Children Learning to Write: Can Novices Be Masters?" *Cognition and Instruction,* 1993, 10, 281–333.

Dominowski, R. L. "Verbalization and Problem Solving." In D. J. Hacker, J. Dunlosky, and A. C. Graesser (eds.), *Metacognition in Educational Theory and Practice.* Hillsdale, N.J.: Erlbaum, 1998, pp. 25–46.

Edney, R. K. "Great Expectations." *Pennsylvania CPA Journal,* 1991, 61(3), 12–16.

Evensen, D. H., Salisbury-Glennon, J. D., and Glenn, J. "A Qualitative Study of Six Medical Students in a Problem-Based Curriculum: Toward a Situated Model of Self-Regulation." *Journal of Educational Psychology,* 2001, 93(4), 659–676.

Goldsmith, B. "Innovative Problem Solving." *AFP Exchange,* 2001, 21(4), 78–79.

Hersh, R. H. "The Liberal Arts College: The Most Practical and Professional Education for the Twenty-First Century." *Liberal Education,* 1997, 83(3), 26–33.

Hmelo, C. E., and Evensen, D. H. "Introduction to Problem-Based Learning: Gaining Insights on Learning Interactions Through Multiple Methods of Inquiry." In D. H. Evensen and C. E. Hmelo (eds.), *Problem-Based Learning: A Research Perspective on Learning Interactions.* Mahwah, N.J.: Erlbaum, 2000, pp. 1–16.

Hmelo, C. E., and Lin, X. "Becoming Self-Directed Learners: Strategy Development in Problem-Based Learning." In D. H. Evensen and C. E. Hmelo (eds.), *Problem-Based Learning: A Research Perspective on Learning Interactions.* Mahwah, N.J.: Erlbaum, 2000, pp. 227–250.

Holmes, A. F. *The Idea of a Christian College.* (rev. ed.) Grand Rapids, Mich.: Eerdman's, 1996.

Jonassen, D. H. "Toward a Design Theory of Problem Solving." *Educational Technology Research and Development,* 2000, *48*(4), 63–85.

Jonassen, D. H. "Engaging and Supporting Problem Solving in Online Learning." *Quarterly Review of Distance Education,* 2002, *3*(1), 1–13.

Kaufman, D. M., and Mann, K. V. "Students' Perceptions About Their Courses in Problem-Based Learning and Conventional Curricula." *Academic Medicine,* 1996, *71*(1), S52–S54.

Lang, E. M. "Distinctively American: The Liberal Arts College." *Daedalus,* 1999, *128*(1), 133–150.

Lindemann, E. *A Rhetoric for Writing Teachers.* (3rd ed.) New York: Oxford University Press, 1995.

Speck, B. W. "Challenging the Validity of Students' Ethical Relativism." *Perspectives,* 1997, *27*(1), 55–70.

Whiteley, S. "The Society Responds to Employer Expectations." *CMA Magazine,* 1993, *67*(6), 2.

Williams, B. "The Theoretical Links Between Problem-Based Learning and Self-Directed Learning for Continuing Professional Nursing Education." *Teaching in Higher Education,* 2001, *6*(1), 85–98.

Zorn, T. "Converging with Divergence: Overcoming the Disciplinary Fragmentation in Business Communication, Organizational Communication, and Public Relations." *Business Communication Quarterly,* 2002, *65*(2), 44–53.

DAVE S. KNOWLTON *is assistant professor of instructional technology in the department of educational leadership at Southern Illinois University Edwardsville.*

2

Professors who wish to implement problem-based learning (PBL) must reconcile numerous tensions regarding its efficacy. The authors address some of these tensions by considering empirical literature about PBL.

Exploring the Tensions of Problem-Based Learning: Insights from Research

Woei Hung, Jessica Harpole Bailey, David H. Jonassen

Researchers have considered many design and development issues related to problem-based learning (PBL). Because PBL is a relatively new and innovative form of instruction, though, much of this research seems contradictory and has created tensions for professors who plan to design and implement PBL activities. In this article, we examine five of these tensions that may be of concern to professors: depth versus breadth of curriculum, higher-order thinking versus factual knowledge acquisition, long-term effects versus immediate learning outcomes, traditional roles of professors versus the roles of PBL tutors, and students' initial discomforts versus their positive attitudes. As we discuss each of these tensions, we offer insights into these tensions as described in the empirical research on PBL. Although these insights do not necessarily offer quick and easy resolutions, we at least raise various perspectives for professors' consideration as they attempt to implement PBL.

Depth Versus Breadth of Curriculum

Critics may argue that PBL focuses on relatively finite problems that require students to consider only limited content; therefore, the PBL method limits the possibility of students being exposed to broader content that may be a part of a course or program of studies but may not be directly related to the causes or solutions of the problem under investigation. This argument that PBL sacrifices breadth for depth seems intuitively reasonable. After all, the steps of problem solving are likely to focus on microelements of course content. Furthermore, the problem-solving processes of engaging in collaboration to explore a problem, determining an appropriate course of action through negotiation and research, and testing solutions are time-consuming.

PBL supporters might respond to this criticism by noting that the depth is purposeful; as students explore content more deeply, they are more likely to develop an in-depth understanding of content that would be sacrificed by focusing on breadth. Numerous studies support the perspective that PBL promotes more in-depth understanding of content than traditional methods (Coles, 1985; Dods, 1997; Newble and Clarke, 1986). How does depth of focus result in an in-depth understanding of content? One explanation for this phenomenon may be that PBL increases students' interest in the content being studied. Increased interest seems evident based on Lieux's (1996) study of PBL class attendance, which was significantly higher than attendance in a lecture class. Increased interest leads to stronger engagement in learning (Norman and Schmidt, 1992), which in turn may result in more in-depth understanding. Also, problem solving is a goal-directed activity (Schank, Fano, Bell, and Jona, 1993/1994). Focusing on the goal of solving a problem is more likely to promote in-depth understanding than simply "covering" a breadth of content.

Another explanation of why PBL seems to foster a depth of understanding may be connected to higher motivation among students. MacKinnon (1999) observed that students in PBL courses were motivated because PBL created a sense of classroom community throughout the learning process and allowed students to take control of the problem that they were attempting to solve. Furthermore, motivation might result when the problems that students attempt to solve are relevant to their personal needs. Because of this sense of ownership and relevance, students are likely to pursue more deeply issues surrounding a problem and potential solution.

Our consideration of the tension between depth and breadth leads us to note that PBL is time-consuming and inherently focuses on a range of content that is relevant to the problems that students are solving. Furthermore, we assert that stronger engagement and higher motivation lead to a stronger likelihood that students will engage in learning that promotes depth over breadth. This analysis leads us to two questions that professors might ask themselves as they consider implementing PBL. The first is simple: What's wrong with pursuing depth as opposed to breadth? Knowledge is constantly expanding, and we question the possibility that any course, or program of studies, can provide students with a full understanding of a content's breadth. If we are right, then we are calling into question the possibility that breadth is a viable strategy for educating students, and we are raising questions about the assumption that more content equals a better education. Our second question relates to the possibility for balance between depth and breadth: Is less breadth an inevitable trade-off for gaining a more in-depth understanding of content? If yes, then what is the optimal balance between depth and breadth, given time constraints? If no, how can depth and breadth complement and add value to each other?

Higher-Order Thinking Versus Factual Knowledge Acquisition

PBL is often praised for its emphasis on higher-order thinking among students. But this emphasis seems to come at the expense of factual knowledge acquisition. Both professors and students have expressed concerns about the lack of knowledge acquisition that occurs in PBL environments (Lieux, 1996; Schultz-Ross and Kline, 1999). But are these concerns valid?

Gallagher and Stepien (1996) conducted a study to investigate the issue. They administered a sixty-five-item multiple-choice test to students in both PBL and non-PBL American studies courses. They administered the test near the end of the courses to best simulate a typical final exam. The results showed no significant difference in content acquisition between students in the PBL class and those in the non-PBL class. Other researchers found similar results in a course on quantity food production and service (Lieux, 1996) and in a summer school program designed to improve students' knowledge about diabetes (Schlundt and others, 1999).

Researchers have conducted similar studies in medical education, where students' performance on the National Board of Medical Examination (NBME) is a primary measure of knowledge acquisition. Albanese and Mitchell (1993) and Vernon and Blake (1993) conducted comprehensive meta-analyses that considered over twenty years of literature dealing with PBL in medical education. Both analyses revealed that students who studied basic science through traditional means performed better in basic science knowledge acquisition (NBME Part 1) than did students who studied basic science in a PBL environment, whereas PBL students performed better than students from traditional formats in clinical knowledge acquisition (NBME Part 2). Berkson (1993) and Colliver (2000) conducted PBL literature reviews that did not agree completely with the results of the two meta-analyses. Their findings indicated similar achievement among students in traditional and PBL groups. Therefore, they concluded that PBL caused no harm in students' learning performance.

Blake, Hosokawa, and Riley (2000) reported on an implementation of PBL as a major component of the medical school curriculum at the University of Missouri-Columbia. They compared the performances of six classes (from 1995 to 1999) on the United States Medical Licensing Examination (USMLE, formerly NBME). The 1995 and 1996 classes were under the traditional curriculum, and the 1997–1999 classes were under the new PBL curriculum. They found that the classes from the PBL curriculum performed substantially better than the classes from the traditional curriculum in both basic science (USMLE Step 1) and clinical knowledge (USMLE Step 2). Furthermore, the classes from the traditional curriculum scored below the national mean, and the difference between the mean score of the 1996 class and the national mean was statistically significant. In contrast, the mean scores of the classes from the PBL curriculum were above the national mean, and the differences between the national mean and the mean scores of the 1998 and 1999 classes were statistically significant.

Our review of PBL research suggests that concerns about PBL sacrificing knowledge acquisition are unwarranted. In fact, the studies that we cite in this section suggest that higher-order thinking and knowledge acquisition can coexist and even bolster each other. These studies should provide some comfort for professors who are considering implementing PBL but are concerned about the degree to which students will acquire factual knowledge.

Long-Term Effects Versus Immediate Learning Outcomes

A primary goal of PBL is to prepare students to be self-directed, lifelong learners and practical problem solvers. Creating tension with this goal, though, is the need to prepare students for short-term assessments, such as standardized tests that may not focus on practical problems. In medical education, this tension casts some doubt on PBL's efficacy in preparing medical students for the USMLE. In liberal arts programs, professors may shy away from PBL because of concerns about preparing students for the Graduate Record Examinations or program exit exams. Seemingly, the idea of educating students to be lifelong self-directed learners and real-world problem solvers contrasts with the need to prepare students for standardized tests. As we have already noted, though, to some extent, this tension has little basis in the literature. PBL does not harm students in their attempt to acquire factual knowledge that may be useful on tests.

But some evidence suggests that although PBL fosters better retention of knowledge over a longer period of time, it may lessen students' initial acquisition of knowledge (Norman and Schmidt, 1992). Even if the literature supporting the view that PBL damages students' short-term knowledge acquisition is scant, we would be inattentive to use PBL in situations where immediate knowledge acquisition is needed unless we can show that the benefits are worth the cost. Does PBL have long-term positive effects on problem-solving skills and transference of those skills to real-world settings? We review research that addresses these questions; then we draw some conclusions regarding this tension between long-term benefits and possible short-term costs.

Problem-Solving Skills. Students who are effective in solving ill-structured problems are able to articulate the problem scope (Newell and Simon, 1972), use critical-thinking skills to evaluate information (Chrispeels and Martin, 1998), and use metacognitive skills to reflect on their own problem-solving process (Barrows and Myers, 1993). At least some research supports the view that PBL can enhance students' problem-solving abilities. To examine the effect of PBL on problem-solving skill, Gallagher, Stepien, and Rosenthal (1992) tested students before and after they enrolled in an interdisciplinary PBL course and a comparison group of students. These tests focused on students' uses of the steps for solving problems in course exercises. They found differences between the two groups. The comparison group tended to skip "problem finding" and move directly from "fact finding" to implementation during the posttest. Conversely, PBL students showed a significant increase in including problem-finding steps in their problem-solving processes. These results suggest that the PBL course was effective in shaping students' problem-solving processes.

Problem-Solving Transfer. PBL shows a positive effect on students' abilities to transfer problem-solving skills from the classroom to real-world situations. Lohman and Finkelstein (1999) found that first-year dental students in a ten-month PBL program improved significantly in the transfer of problem-solving skills. Similarly, graduates from a PBL chemical engineering program were praised for their outstanding problem-solving skills and job performance. Other new employees of the same organization needed to be trained for up to one and a half years to be able to solve problems independently (Woods, 1996). Because students are able to transfer their problem-solving skills to the real world, they are more likely to be successful as self-directed learners (Norman and Schmidt, 1992).

Conclusions Regarding the Tension. In the past two subsections, we have pointed to evidence that PBL has strong positive effects in promoting students' problem-solving skills and their ability to transfer these skills to real-world situations. We offer this evidence in light of concerns that PBL may negatively affect students' performance on tests. We recognize that some professors necessarily may be concerned about students' performances on tests, but given the scant evidence that PBL damages students' performances on tests, we suggest that the benefits of PBL outweigh the costs in regard to this tension. In fact, we argue that through the proper design of PBL environments that includes instruction facilitating the ability of students to develop expert-like mental models for solving problems, professors can adequately prepare students for both long- and short-term success.

Students' Initial Discomfort Versus Their Positive Attitudes

Students find the initial transitions into PBL to be difficult. Ultimately, though, they become generally satisfied with PBL. In this section, we discuss students' frustrations with initial transitions to PBL and their satisfaction with PBL once the transition is made. After considering students' contrasting views, we offer ideas to professors on how to assist students with a smooth transition into PBL.

Frustrations of Transition to PBL. Research shows that the initial transition from a traditional to a PBL curriculum may be a difficult adjustment for students. The adjustment is difficult because, as we discussed in the earlier section on depth versus breadth, students are concerned about content coverage in PBL environments (Dods, 1997; Lieux, 1996). Their concerns also relate to uncertainty about their grades (Woods, 1996).

Another reason for students' frustrations might be the newness of students' roles in PBL. On average, students are not self-directed; that is, they have never been required to initiate inquiry and problem-solving processes. Unfortunately, students' lack of self-directedness is a common residue from studying under traditional instructional methods. Fiddler and Knoll (1995) seem to confirm this contention. They reported that dissatisfaction and frustration during the initial stages of PBL were due to the absence of a predefined cognitive framework that students could follow and use throughout the learning process. In traditional classrooms, professors usually provide such a framework, and students passively receive that framework. In PBL, though, the students become the initiators of their own learning, the inquirers, and the problem solvers during the learning process. This shift requires the students not only to adjust their own learning style but also to redefine their roles in the learning process. The difficulty of adjusting themselves to taking a more active role and more responsibilities in the learning process could be again tied to the students' "learned" definition of roles in traditional methods (Jost, Harvard, and Smith, 1997; Dean, 1999).

More interestingly, Lieux (1996) observed an inconsistency between the students' perceptions of their work and their actual performance. Based on the students' evaluation of the course using the Instructional Development and Effectiveness Assessment (IDEA), Lieux found that the PBL group perceived that they had learned less than the lecture group. However, the results of the students' final examinations did not agree with their perceptions about learning. The two groups of students did equally well in their final exam.

Post-Transition Satisfaction. Although discomfort is common among students in the initial stage of PBL implementation, Schultz-Ross and Kline (1999) found that students' discomfort and dissatisfaction levels decreased significantly at the end of a PBL forensic psychiatry course. On the whole, research indicates that students are generally satisfied with PBL curriculum (Caplow, Donaldson, Kardash, and Hosokawa, 1997; Dods, 1997; Fiddler and Knoll, 1995). Vernon and Blake's (1993) meta-analysis of thirty-five studies comparing PBL with traditional instructional methods revealed that students' attitudes and opinions about their PBL programs were significantly higher than their counterparts in the traditional curriculum. The results of this analysis and other studies (for example, Kaufman and Mann, 1996; Woods, 1996) suggest a trend that students favor PBL over traditional instructional method and curriculum.

What, specifically, did the students like about PBL? Students find PBL conducive to promoting social interaction, and they generally view PBL as an effective instructional method. Regarding the promotion of social skills, Lieux (1996) reported that PBL students perceived themselves as gaining substantial effectiveness in communication skills and a stronger sense of personal responsibility, whereas the students in the lecture section did not share the same perception. Students in Dean's (1999) study perceived an increase of confidence in working within teams. Martin, Chrispeels, and D'eidio-Caston (1998) reported that students recognized improvement in their own listening skills and in their ability to identify group-member skills that promoted group effectiveness.

In addition, students found PBL to be an effective instructional method. Bernstein, Tipping, Bercovitz, and Skinner (1995) administered open-ended questionnaires to medical students at the beginning of a PBL class and five weeks after studying in the PBL class. The results indicated a significant increase in the attitudes from pretest to posttest in the area of students' perceptions of PBL as an effective method of learning. Similar results were obtained in Schultz-Ross and Kline's (1999) study of using PBL to teach forensic psychiatry. Other studies have shown that students considered PBL to be effective in enhancing their confidence in judging alternatives for solving problems (Dean, 1999), helping them acquire social study content (Shepherd, 1998), improving their learning of basic science information (Caplow, Donaldson, Kardash, and Hosokawa, 1997), and developing thinking and problem-solving skills (Lieux, 1996).

Assisting Students with a Smooth Transition. The inconsistency between students' initial and longer-term perceptions suggests that professors must help students make a smooth transition to PBL. Because PBL is a radical shift for students who are accustomed to traditional methods, professors must make explicit students' roles and responsibilities within a PBL framework. For example, professors might consider offering descriptions of PBL within a course syllabus. Professors might even consider sharing with students the reactions of other students who have learned in PBL environments.

Traditional Role of Professors Versus the Roles of PBL Tutors

Maudsley (1999) suggests that PBL requires professors to reposition their roles in teaching from a transmitter of knowledge and information to a facilitator of thinking and learning. Professors who have experience teaching in a traditional lecture-based format may be uncomfortable with this repositioning from lecturer to facilitator—or "tutor," to use the language of PBL. The lack of comfort may be particularly acute for professors who desire control of classrooms and prefer passive students (Margetson, 1991). In addition, professors who view knowledge as a body of information that should be transmitted from knowledgeable teachers to students may also feel threatened by the PBL teaching method. In fact, Kaufman and Holmes (1998) found that PBL tutors who are content experts have a more difficult time with the role of tutor.

PBL tutors should control their discomfort and avoid lecturing (Maudsley, 1999) or taking control of classroom processes. To do so is to undermine PBL. To help professors consider the benefits of giving up lecturing in the name of being an effective tutor, we offer three components of effective PBL tutoring. We hope a discussion of these components helps skeptic professors reconsider the merits of facilitating problem solving, as opposed to attempting to fill students with knowledge.

Cognitive Congruence. Cognitive congruence is "the ability to express oneself in the language of the students, using the concepts they use and explaining things in ways easily grasped by students" (Schmidt and Moust, 1995, p. 709). Effective communication with students is essential if tutors are to successfully guide the students' learning processes throughout PBL. Moreover, the authenticity of tutors' interaction is exhibited in their ability to communicate with students informally while maintaining an empathetic attitude. Some research suggests that when tutors are not actively engaged in guiding students in a cognitively congruent way, students feel that their learning experiences suffer (Martin, Chrispeels, and D'eidio-Caston, 1998).

Metacognitive and Self-Directed-Learning Model. By modeling problem-solving processes and metacognitive thinking, professors can serve as a concrete example for students. By observing examples, students are more likely to develop the needed skills. As metacognitive models, PBL tutors helped promote the development of clinical reasoning skills in surgery students (Mayo, Donnelly, Nash, and Schwartz, 1993). Although not giving answers, the tutors modeled questions that an expert physician might ask in a clinical case. These questions guide students to raise questions indicative of those that an expert physician might raise. Wilkerson's (1995) findings seem to support the importance of tutors as metacognitive models. Students deemed tutors as effective and helpful when they modeled expert physicians' reasoning process. (For more about metacognition, see Chapter Ten of this volume.)

Group Processing Skills. Believing that outstanding tutors "possess a distinct and subtle group of skills," Mayo, Donnelly, Nash, and Schwartz (1993, p. 227) designed a study to identify those skills. Results revealed four consequential, yet broad, tutor skills: promoting group awareness of its own processes, encouraging feedback within groups, assisting groups with setting appropriate learning issues, and guiding groups toward integrating learning issues. Similarly, De Grave, Dolmans, and van der Vleuten (1999) used the Tutor Intervention Profile to assess the effectiveness of PBL tutors and found that enhancing learning processes within groups was one of the characteristics that students valued. Because working in groups is one of the distinct characteristics of PBL, tutors must be able to facilitate productive collaborative relationships (Wilkerson, 1995) and an unthreatening working atmosphere (Schmidt and Moust, 1995).

Conclusions and Implications

Our purpose in this article has been to raise numerous tensions that typically are considered by both critics and advocates of PBL. We believe that the PBL method may change the nature of education. But for this to happen, professors must come to terms with and find ways to ease those tensions. Only then will higher education recognize the full potential of PBL to promote lifelong, self-directed learning among students.

References

Albanese, M. A., and Mitchell, S. "Problem-Based Learning: A Review of Literature on Its Outcomes and Implementation Issues." *Academic Medicine*, 1993, *68*, 52–81.

Barrows, H. S., and Myers, A. C. "Problem Based Learning in Secondary Schools." Unpublished monograph. Springfield, Ill.: Problem Based Learning Institute, Lanphier High School, and Southern Illinois University Medical School, 1993.

Berkson, L. "Problem-Based Learning: Have the Expectations Been Met?" *Academic Medicine*, 1993, *68*, S79–S88.

Bernstein, P., Tipping, J., Bercovitz, K., and Skinner, H. A. "Shifting Students and Faculty to a PBL Curriculum: Attitudes Changed and Lessons Learned." *Academic Medicine*, 1995, *70*, 245–247.

Blake, R. L., Hosokawa, M. C., and Riley, S. L. "Student Performances on Step 1 and Step 2 of the United States Medical Licensing Examination Following Implementation of a Problem-Based Learning Curriculum." *Academic Medicine*, 2000, *75*, 66–70.

Caplow, J. H., Donaldson, J. F., Kardash, C. A., and Hosokawa, M. "Learning in a Problem-Based Medical Curriculum: Students' Conceptions." *Medical Education*, 1997, *31*, 1–8.

Chrispeels, J. H., and Martin, K. J. "Becoming Problem Solvers: The Case of Three Future Administrators." *Journal of School Leadership*, 1998, *8*, 303–331.

Coles, C. R. "Differences Between Conventional and Problem-Based Curricula in Their Students' Approaches to Studying." *Medical Education*, 1985, *19*, 308–309.

Colliver, J. A. "Effectiveness of Problem-Based Learning Curricula: Research and Theory." *Academic Medicine*, 2000, *75*(3), 259–266.

De Grave, W. S., Dolmans, D.H.J.M., and van der Vleuten, C.P.M. "Profiles of Effective Tutors in Problem-Based Learning: Scaffolding Student Learning." *Medical Education*, 1999, *33*, 901–906.

Dean, C. D. "Problem-Based Learning in Teacher Education." Paper presented at the annual meeting of American Educational Research Association, Montreal, Quebec, 1999. (ED 431 771)

Dods, R. F. "An Action Research Study of the Effectiveness of Problem-Based Learning in Promoting the Acquisition and Retention of Knowledge." *Journal for the Education of the Gifted*, 1997, *20*, 423–437.

Dunlap, J. C. "The Relationship of Problem-Based Learning to Life-Long Learning." Doctoral dissertation, University of Colorado at Denver, 1996. *Dissertation Abstracts International*, 1996, *58*, 71A.

Eisenstaedt, R. S., Barry, W. E., and Glanz, K. "Problem-Based Learning: Cognitive Retention and Cohort Traits of Randomly Selected Participants and Decliners." *Academic Medicine*, 1990, *65*, 511–512.

Fiddler, M. B., and Knoll, J. W. "Problem-Based Learning in an Adult Liberal Learning Context: Learner Adaptations and Feedback." *Continuing Higher Education Review*, 1995, *59*(1/2), 13, 24.

Gallagher, S. A., and Stepien, W. J. "Content Acquisition in Problem-Based Learning: Depth Versus Breadth in American Studies." *Journal for the Education of the Gifted,* 1996, *19,* 257–275.

Gallagher, S. A., Stepien, W. J., and Rosenthal, H. "The Effects of Problem-Based Learning on Problem Solving." *Gifted Child Quarterly,* 1992, *36*(4), 195–200.

Jost, K. L., Harvard, B. C., and Smith, A. J. "A Study of Problem-Based Learning in a Graduate Education Classroom." In Proceedings of Selected Research and Development Presentation at the National Convention of the Association for Educational Communications and Technology, 19th, Albuquerque, Feb. 1997. (ED 409 840)

Kaufman, D. M., and Holmes, D. B. "The Relationship of Tutors' Content Expertise to Interventions and Perceptions in a PBL Medical Curriculum." *Medical Education,* 1998, *32,* 255–261.

Kaufman, D. M., and Mann, K. V. "Students' Perceptions About Their Courses in Problem-Based Learning and Conventional Curricula." *Academic Medicine,* 1996, *71*(1), S52–S54.

Lieux, E. M. "A Comparative Study of Learning in Lecture Vs. Problem-Based Format." *About Teaching—#50.* A Newsletter of the Center for Teaching Effectiveness, Spring 1996, University of Delaware. [http://www.udel.edu/pbl/cte/spr96-nutr.html].

Lohman, M. C., and Finkelstein, M. "Segmenting Information in PBL Cases to Foster the Development of Problem-Solving Skill, Self-Directedness, and Technical Knowledge." Unpublished manuscript, Florida State University and University of Iowa, 1999.

MacKinnon, M. M. "CORE Elements of Student Motivation in Problem-Based Learning." In M. Theall (ed.), *Motivation from Within: Approaches for Encouraging Faculty and Students to Excel.* New Directions for Teaching and Learning, no. 78. San Francisco: Jossey-Bass, 1999, pp. 49–58.

Margetson, D. "Why Is Problem-Based Learning a Challenge?" In D. Boud and G. Felitti (eds.), *The Challenge of Problem-Based Learning.* New York: St. Martin's Press, 1991, pp. 42–50.

Martin, K. J., Chrispeels, J. H., and D'eidio-Caston, M. "Exploring the Use of Problem-Based Learning for Developing Collaborative Leadership Skills." *Journal of School Leadership,* 1998, *8,* 470–500.

Maudsley, G. "Roles and Responsibilities of the Problem-Based Tutor in the Undergraduate Medical Curriculum." *British Medical Journal,* 1999, *318*(169), 657–661.

Mayo, P., Donnelly, M. B., Nash, P. P., and Schwartz, R. W. "Student Perceptions of Tutor Effectiveness in a Problem-Based Surgery Clerkship." *Teaching and Learning in Medicine,* 1993, *5*(4), 227–233.

Newble, D. I., and Clarke, R. M. "The Approaches to Learning of Students in a Traditional and in an Innovative Problem-Based Medical School." *Medical Education,* 1986, *20,* 267–273.

Newell, A., and Simon, H. A. *Human Problem Solving.* Englewood Cliffs, N.J.: Prentice Hall, 1972.

Norman, G. R., and Schmidt, H. G. "The Psychological Basis of Problem-Based Learning: A Review of the Evidence." *Academic Medicine,* 1992, *67*(9), 557–565.

Schank, R. C., Fano, A., Bell, B., and Jona, M. "The Design of Goal-Based Scenarios." *Journal of the Learning Science,* 1993/1994, *3,* 305–345.

Schlundt, D. G., and others. "Evaluation of a Multicomponent, Behaviorally Oriented, Problem-Based 'Summer School' Program for Adolescents with Diabetes." *Behavior Modification,* 1999, *23*(1), 79–105.

Schmidt, H. G., and Moust, J.H.C. "What Makes a Tutor Effective? A Structural-Equations Modeling Approach to Learning in Problem-Based Curricula." *Academic Medicine,* 1995, *70*(8), 708–714.

Schultz-Ross, R. A., and Kline, A. E. "Using Problem-Based Learning to Teach Forensic Psychiatry." *Academic Psychiatry*, 1999, *23*, 37–41.

Shepherd, N. G. "The Probe Method: A Problem-Based Learning Model's Effect on Critical Thinking Skills of Fourth and Fifth Grade Social Studies Students." Doctoral dissertation, North Carolina State University. *Dissertation Abstracts International*, 1998, *59*, 779A.

Vernon, D.T.A., and Blake, R. L. "Does Problem-Based Learning Work: A Meta-Analysis of Evaluative Research." *Academic Medicine*, 1993, *68*, 550–563.

Wilkerson, L. "Identification of Skills for the Problem-Based Tutor: Student and Faculty Perspectives." *Instructional Science*, 1995, *22*, 303–315.

Woods, D. R. "Problem-Based Learning for Large Classes in Chemical Engineering." In L. Wilkerson and W. H. Gijselaers (eds.), *Bringing Problem-Based Learning to Higher Education: Theory and Practice*. New Directions for Teaching and Learning, no. 68. San Francisco: Jossey-Bass, 1996, 91–99.

WOEI HUNG is a doctoral student in information science and learning technologies at the University of Missouri–Columbia.

JESSICA HARPOLE BAILEY is assistant professor of health information management at the University of Mississippi Medical Center in Jackson.

DAVID H. JONASSEN is distinguished professor in information science and learning technologies at the University of Missouri–Columbia.

The design of the problem can be a key to success in using problem-based learning. This chapter discusses characteristics of effective problems that will elicit higher-order thinking among students.

Designing Problems to Promote Higher-Order Thinking

Renée E. Weiss

A crucial aspect of problem-based learning (PBL) is the actual design of the problem to be solved (Jonassen, 2000). Without a carefully designed problem, professors may believe that they are inspiring students to analyze, research, and solve problems; in reality, though, they may only be using a simple problem with a well-defined solution, which results in a scavenger hunt for information from resources that the professor has provided (White, 2001).

Designing a problem for higher-order thinking may seem like a daunting task for a professor who is unfamiliar with PBL. However, in this article, I describe two stages for designing a PBL problem. In the first stage, professors must consider the educational purpose of the problem. In the second stage, professors must design the problem to meet the intended purpose. After discussing these two stages, I offer practical examples of problems and discuss how they meet the criteria for a well-designed problem.

Determining the Purpose of the Problem

Professors should have a clear purpose in mind when deciding to use PBL. In other words, professors who use PBL must ask a fundamental question: "What am I trying to accomplish by assigning this problem?" Unless professors address this question, they are likely to end up with problems that do not serve their intended purpose.

Most basically, PBL should enhance and promote the goals of a course or program of studies, not serve as a digression in curriculum and pedagogy. The problem that serves as a basis of PBL activity, then, should promote students' knowledge and skills that have been clearly defined as intended course or program outcomes (Barrows, 1996; Drummond-Young and Mohide, 2001).

Duffy and Cunningham (1996) offer five purposes for implementing problems: guiding; testing; illustrating principles, concepts, or procedures; fostering the processing of content; and providing a stimulus for activity. First, professors might use a problem simply to guide students toward certain content or approaches. In other words, the problem is designed simply to focus the students' attention toward salient course concepts. Second, a problem may serve as a test. When professors use problems as tests, they are creating a situation where students must apply course knowledge. Sometimes these problem-tests are simplistic, such as addressing exercises from the end of a textbook chapter. Third, a problem can be used to illustrate the principle, concept, or procedure that is the focus of the problem. In this respect, professors introduce problems for students to solve as an alternative to lecture. Instead of the professor explaining a principle, defining a concept, or guiding students through procedures, professors assign problems that will force students to inductively discover explanations, definitions, and processes. Fourth, problems can serve as a vehicle for promoting thoughtfulness among students. In this case, professors are using problems primarily as a basis to stimulate and train thinking skills. Fifth, problems may serve as stimuli for activity. This fifth purpose is the most ambiguous for assigning problems to students. The notion of stimulating activity is broad, and students might engage in a variety of activities to solve the problem. A well-designed problem that meets this fifth purpose will force students to think on high levels as they struggle to bring order to the ambiguity.

Designing Problems to Promote Higher Activity

As I have pointed out, PBL problems can serve a variety of purposes. All of these purposes have some merit, but the highest purpose of PBL in general is to stimulate student activity and engagement. In this section, I suggest criteria for a problem that will stimulate activity—and thus higher thinking—among students.

Appropriate for Students. A good problem should be based on an analysis of students' current content knowledge. If a problem is to serve as a stimulus for higher-order and critical thinking, students must find the problem to be challenging (Duch, 2001). Therefore, professors should assess students' current knowledge of the content inherent to a problem and design that problem slightly beyond what students currently know. As a result, students will not be able to solve the problem without slightly extending their knowledge base and their skills. This extension will move students beyond simply regurgitating what they already know; they will have to develop a deeper (or broader) understanding of the content to solve the problem at hand (Duch, 2001).

Ill Structured. Closely allied to this issue of appropriateness for students is the issue of problem structure. Jonassen (2000) notes that problems generally can be characterized as either well structured or ill structured. Well-structured problems can guide students toward salient processes in a course and can be effective for demonstrating simple rules, concepts, and procedures. The solutions to well-structured problems are ones the learners can find from limited sources.

Ill-structured problems, on the other hand, are messy like the problems that are faced in everyday life and in professional practice (Delisle, 1997; Duch, 2001; Jonassen, 2000). Not all the elements of the problem are known, and ill-structured problems possess several solutions or perhaps no solution. Ill-structured problems also are not confined by discipline boundaries (Stinson and Milter, 1996), so students may need to draw from a number of different fields to solve the problem.

If the professor's goal in designing the problem is to foster higher-order activity among students, then the problem should be relatively ill structured. The distinction is important because recent research has thrown into question the assumption that learning to solve well-structured problems will facilitate the ability to solve ill-structured problems (Jonassen, 2000).

Collaborative. Problems designed to promote higher-order thinking should require collaboration among students (Gijselaers, 1996). Sometimes when professors design collaborative assignments, students each complete a part of the assignment, and then they assemble the parts for submission to the professor. This puzzle-piecing approach is not sufficient in a PBL assignment where the problem is designed to foster higher-order thinking among students (Drummond-Young and Mohide, 2001; Duch, 2001). Rather, professors should design the problem so that the group must synthesize their ideas and make decisions throughout the course of the PBL activity.

Allen, Duch, and Groh (1996) go beyond arguing that strong problems require collaboration. They suggest that viable problems for promoting higher-order thinking engender controversy among members of the group. The acts of synthesizing ideas, making decisions, and resolving controversy will require students to socially negotiate learning issues inherent to the problem and defend among themselves the feasibility of those solutions (Duch, 2001).

Authentic. As professors consider authentic slants to problems that serve as the basis of PBL, they should be aware of two aspects of authenticity. First, in some respects, the problem is authentic only if it is grounded in students' experiences. That is, if a problem is too theoretical and out of touch with students' experiences and daily lives, they will not be engaged by the problem (Delisle, 1997; Mayer, 1998).

Second, even if a problem is not based in students' current experiences, it may be authentic if it relates to students' future plans and expected careers (Delisle, 1997; Stinson and Milter, 1996). PBL problems should be more than theoretical exercises. Professors should design problems that require students to apply content in ways indicative of emerging professionals.

Promotes Lifelong and Self-Directed Learning. To some extent, a problem that meets the other criteria offered in this section will likely motivate students to become lifelong and self-directed learners. That is, if a problem is appropriate for learners, authentic, and requires collaboration, then students will feel empowered and understand the ways that problem-solving skills can benefit them throughout life.

Examining two of these criteria can provide insights into the connection among lifelong learning, self-directed learning, and other criteria offered in this section. A problem that is authentic is likely to encourage lifelong problem solving and self-directed learning. When students solve a problem that is of real interest to them, they will probably find their own solutions to be inadequate. Therefore, they are more likely to become self-directed learners and pursue further analysis of and alternative solutions to the problem.

Furthermore, as students work collaboratively, they likely will assimilate a variety of approaches toward solving problems. That is, students learn from each other how to solve problems. Because of this type of assimilation, each student will learn new and novel—at least to that student—approaches for acquiring knowledge and solving problems (Barrows, 1996; Gijselaers, 1996). Students can use these new approaches throughout life.

Examples of PBL Problems

Numerous examples of PBL problems might be helpful for promoting a better understanding of problem design. After each example, I offer an analysis of the problem in light of characteristics of good problems for higher-order thinking.

Example Problem One. The following problem might be indicative of a case-based problem given to first-year ophthalmology students:

> A sixty-year-old man complains of murky vision. He also says that when he reads, he sees only parts of letters. In reviewing the patient's case, you discover a history of retinal disease in his family. Also, you discover that he has had some symptoms of neurological disease, diabetes, and hematological problems.
>
> Before you leave class tonight, you must address the following questions: First, from what you have learned about retinal disease, which is most relevant to the goal of correctly diagnosing and treating the patient, the history of neurological disease, diabetes, or hematological problems? Second, after your group agrees on one answer in the first question, determine some resulting learning issues that need to be researched to diagnose this patient's problem.

Based on the decisions that your group makes tonight, you should devise a plan for researching the various issues. Two weeks from tonight, your group will present a diagnosis based on the issues that you determined as relevant. Based on this diagnosis, you will recommend an appropriate form of treatment or further diagnostic tests that you would need to conduct to determine treatment.

An examination of this problem reveals several characteristics that will promote higher-order thinking among students. We can assume that the problem is appropriately ill structured for ophthalmology students because no one clear path exists toward a diagnosis. In fact, it is unclear that students will even have enough information to make a diagnosis, as opposed to suggesting further testing to determine a diagnosis. Because of this ill structure, the students in the group must collaboratively make decisions about the steps for solving this problem. This ill-structured nature of the problem also gives it an authenticity because ophthalmologists must diagnose patients' disorders and determine regimens for treatment.

Example Problem Two. The following problem might be one given to students in a first-year undergraduate advertising course.

Smalltown is one of the fastest growing towns in the area. It prides itself on its new bike trail that includes paved areas and beautifully landscaped natural settings. According to the Smalltown police chief, the bike trails are the target of vandals who have painted graffiti on the asphalt trail and on trees in more scenic and natural parts of the trail. Furthermore, the bike trails are constantly littered with empty water bottles, old tires, broken skateboard wheels, and rusty bicycle chains. There have even been two arrests for public drunkenness on the trail. The chamber of commerce has hired you to launch a local advertising campaign that will inspire some civic pride in the trail and develop a sense of community ownership of the trail.

Based on this information, work as a group to reach consensus on the exact nature of the problem, analyze an audience for the advertising campaign that you likely could reach, develop criteria for measuring a "good" campaign for reaching that audience, and develop an outline for three different campaigns that meet your criteria and thus might be successful.

As with the first example problem, this problem requires students to work collaboratively to reach numerous decisions. This problem also is authentic because it requires students to develop an advertising campaign based on careful audience analysis. This problem is ill structured in that there is no one exactly right advertising campaign, and in fact, advertising campaigns might not solve the problem at all. Despite this ambiguity, though, as students work together to define an audience, devise criteria for a successful campaign, and brainstorm ideas for the campaign, they will be engaging in the systematic creative process that they are likely to repeat numerous times throughout their career in the field of advertising.

Summary

Research on learning and cognition has yielded well-grounded principles from which to design PBL problems that promote higher-order thinking among students. In this article, I have discussed some of these principles, and I have provided example problems that contain these principles. The bad news is that there is no step-by-step method for developing a good problem for PBL. The good news is that by paying attention to these characteristics, professors can create problems that are likely to challenge and motivate students.

References

Allen, D. E., Duch, B. J., and Groh, S. E. "The Power of Problem-Based Learning in Teaching Introductory Science Courses." In L. Wilkerson and W. H. Gijselaers (eds.), *Bringing Problem-Based Learning to Higher Education: Theory and Practice.* San Francisco: Jossey-Bass, 1996, pp. 43–52.

Barrows, H. "Problem-Based Learning in Medicine and Beyond: A Brief Overview." In L. Wilkerson and W. H. Gijselaers (eds.), *Bringing Problem-Based Learning to Higher Education: Theory and Practice.* San Francisco: Jossey-Bass, 1996, pp. 3–12.

Delisle, R. *How to Use Problem-Based Learning in the Classroom.* Alexandria, Va.: Association for Supervision and Curriculum Development, 1997.

Drummond-Young, M., and Mohide, E. A. "Developing Problems for Use in Problem-Based Learning." In E. Rideout (ed.), *Transforming Nursing Education Through Problem-Based Learning.* Boston, Mass.: Jones & Bartlett, 2001, pp. 165–191.

Duch, B. J. "Writing Problems for Deeper Understanding." In B. J. Duch, S. E. Groh, and D. E. Allen (eds.), *The Power of Problem-Based Learning: A Practical "How to" for Teaching Undergraduate Courses in Any Discipline.* Sterling, Va.: Stylus, 2001, pp. 47–58.

Duffy, T. M., and Cunningham, D. J. "Constructivism: Implications for the Design and Delivery of Instruction." In D. H. Jonassen (ed.), *Handbook of Research for Educational Communications and Technology.* New York: Simon & Schuster Macmillan, 1996, pp. 170–198.

Gijselaers, W. H. "Connecting Problem-Based Practices with Educational Theory." In L. Wilkerson and W. H. Gijselaers (eds.), *Bringing Problem-Based Learning to Higher Education: Theory and Practice.* New Directions for Teaching and Learning, no. 68. San Francisco: Jossey-Bass, 1996, pp. 13–21.

Jonassen, D. "Toward a Design Theory of Problem Solving." *Educational Technology Research and Development,* 2000, 48(4), 63–85.

Mayer, R. E. "Cognitive, Metacognitive, and Motivational Aspects of Problem Solving." *Instructional Science,* 1998, 26, 49–63.

Stinson, J. E., and Milter, R. G. "Problem-Based Learning in Business Education: Curriculum Design and Implementation Issues." In L. Wilkerson and W. H. Gijselaers (eds.), *Bringing Problem-Based Learning to Higher Education: Theory and Practice.* New Directions for Teaching and Learning, no. 68. San Francisco: Jossey-Bass, 1996, pp. 33–42.

White, H. "Getting Started in Problem-Based Learning." In B. J. Duch, S. E. Groh, and D. E. Allen (eds.), *The Power of Problem-Based Learning: A Practical "How to" for Teaching Undergraduate Courses in Any Discipline.* Sterling, Va.: Stylus, 2001, pp. 69–78.

RENÉE E. WEISS is assistant professor of instructional technology in the department of educational leadership at Southern Illinois University Edwardsville.

4

Professors who want to integrate computers into problem-based learning lessons can use the design model presented in this article. The model is based on a theory of students using computers as problem-solving tools.

Integrating Computers into the Problem-Solving Process

Deborah L. Lowther, Gary R. Morrison

The educational use of computers focuses primarily on the employment of software that ranges from gamelike packages to sophisticated integrated learning systems that provide individualized instruction based on performance. In the workplace, though, computers are used differently than in the educational arena. Computers are used in the workplace to collect, analyze, and communicate information needed to solve problems. For example, population data are collected and analyzed to prepare for future needs, financial data are used to predict spending patterns, and health records are examined to create appropriate treatments and avoid drug interactions.

As a result of this disparity between educational and workplace uses of computers, students often emerge from educational institutions with a limited ability to use computers as tools to solve real-world problems. Green (1999) found that almost 40 percent of the colleges and universities surveyed perceived computer integration as the most important technology-related challenge currently facing American institutions. Yet, whereas college students were found to be adept at e-mail, Internet browsing, and word processing, they lack the knowledge and experience to use problem-solving tools effectively such as spreadsheets and databases (McEuen, 2001). Similarly, Rumbough (1999) found that many college students were unfamiliar with basic computer and Internet components. One solution to this concern is for professors to adopt an inquiry-based approach in which students use computers as problem-solving tools. In this article, we describe a step-by-step approach to assist faculty with designing this type of inquiry-based instruction.

Integrating Technology for Inquiry Model

The concept underlying the INtegrating *Technology* for InQuiry (NTeQ) Model involves the professor, student, lesson, and computer (Morrison and Lowther, 2002). The professor is technologically competent, knowing when and how to effectively integrate the use of computers as a problem-solving tool. The students assume the role of researchers and develop technological competence. The lesson is problem based, and rather than being the focus of learning, the computer is a tool used to collect, analyze, and communicate information.

A ten-step approach is used to plan NTeQ lessons (Figure 4.1). Four of the steps are similar to those used for designing any lesson, and three of the steps are covered in other articles within this volume. We will focus primarily on the five steps of the model that deal specifically with the integration of computers into problem-based environments.

Specify Objectives. The first step in planning a problem-based lesson is to determine the specific learning objectives. In some respects, specifying objectives is tantamount to "determining the purposes of a problem," discussed in Chapter Three of this volume. In specifying objectives, professors select student behaviors that will likely lead to intended student learning.

Match Objectives to Computer Functions. Once the objectives are selected, the next step is to determine if computers can assist with the achievement of the objectives. To make this decision, professors should match the functions of software applications with the learning tasks. Table 4.1 provides useful guidelines for selecting appropriate software for your lesson objectives.

Specify Problem. After establishing what the students are to learn and identifying which computer application(s) can be used to support the learning, professors should develop a problem statement. The problems should be realistic and meaningful to the learner. A more detailed discussion of how to develop a problem can be found in Chapter Three. The following

Figure 4.1. The NTeQ Model

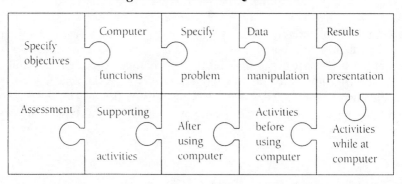

Table 4.1. Software Functions and Usage Guidelines

Software	Functions	When to Use
Database	Store data in records Sort data (alphabetical or numerical) Match data Merge data Create specialized reports	Use with information that has common characteristics and can be easily categorized
Word processing	Edit and format text Create outlines Create columns Generate tables Insert graphics	Use with information that can be paraphrased or organized in meaningful ways
Browser	Search by key words Save favorite Web sites Hyperlink to text, virtual tours, and so forth Provide interactive feedback	Use to access information or to engage in interactive learning
Spreadsheet	Perform calculations Sort data Create graphs and charts	Use with numerical data to analyze and determine trends and outcomes
Communication	Synchronous or asynchronous communication Send and receive text, video, audio, and attachments Store messages	Use when interactivity with others will enhance learning
Concept mapping	Connect ideas Create sequences Add graphics	Use with content that can be categorized, linked, or contrasted
Presentation	Display text Support navigation Create animation Insert or create graphics Insert video and sound	Use to display information that can be enhanced by interactivity

two example problems will be the basis of discussion through the remainder of this article. The first problem could be used in a literature course: "Our class has been hired by the city council. Our task is to work with a team of landscape architects to design a "poet's garden" for the central park of our city" (adapted from Ljung, 1997, p. 5).

The second problem would be appropriate for a health class: "You have been hired as a nutritionist for the leading American long-distance runner for the upcoming Olympics. Your task is to prepare a weekly menu that meets her specified nutritional needs" (adapted from Rasmussen, 1997, p. 8).

Both of these problems are ill structured in that there is not one exact answer that students must find. To solve either of these problems, students must thoroughly examine course content from multiple perspectives to devise meaningful solutions.

Data Manipulation. At this point in the lesson-planning process, the objectives are stated, the types of computer applications are known, and the problem statement is defined. Now it is time to get more specific and designate what data are needed and how the data should be manipulated to solve the problem. This step clarifies whether or not the correct software has been selected.

In designing a poet's garden, students will need a tool to maximize their efficiency in organizing information about the poems they might include in the garden. Because the data to be manipulated are text-based, have repetitive patterns, and contain easily described information, a database is the most appropriate software. The data fields might include poem title, author, author's home country, publication date, flower name, and theme. Once the database is created, students can arrange the information by any field, which might help them identify patterns in the data that could be used as a basis for a garden design. On the other hand, for students developing a menu for the long-distance runner, a spreadsheet would work well as the primary software. Spreadsheets are useful in solving problems regarding calculations, and planning the menu requires multiple calculations, such as totaling calories and determining appropriate dietary ratios of protein, fats, and sugars.

During the actual implementation of the lesson, it is important to *not* provide students with the specific details of what data are needed and how they are to be manipulated. Instead, after introducing the problem statement, engage the students in a brainstorming session to "discover" these components and thus engender a sense of "ownership" regarding the problem's solution.

Results Presentation. Professors must select the final product(s) that will show the problem solution. The computer provides many options for producing these products. For example, students might use word processing to write a report with charts and graphics. Students might make digital presentations with video, animation, or color diagrams. Professors might require students to develop computer-based informational or instructional units. The final product(s) should demonstrate achievement of the specified objectives.

Activities at the Computer. In following the NTeQ model to this point, a professor will have determined the general direction of a lesson, including the way students will present their findings. Now professors can focus on the specific activities in which students will participate. Specifically, professors can plan computer activities, keeping in mind that most lessons will involve more than one type of activity. For example, in creating a poet's garden, students might use four different types of software. Initially, the students might conduct Internet searches for poems with references to flowers and to collect related author information. This information could be placed into a database and manipulated to find patterns for planning the garden. Students could then use a drawing or landscape design program to create the garden design. For the final product, students could create a digital presentation of the garden design displaying color photos of the flowers accompanied by recordings of the poems.

To determine successful computer activities, professors should consider a full range of available software and students' abilities to use that software. If professors think students might need assistance with using the software efficiently, they might consider developing short step-by-step job aids to assist students with specific procedures. When the lesson involves creating a product that is relatively complex, such as a spreadsheet using multiple calculations, professors might consider developing a prototype. By creating a prototype, professors can ensure that the lesson design is workable. Professors might consider showing the prototypes to students as an example of what can be created.

Activities Before Using the Computer. After the computer activities have been planned, professors must determine how students can get prepared to work at the computer. This preparation not only saves time at the computer but also helps students to remain focused on the problem and a solution. Professors might consider designing work sheets that will guide students' thinking as they clarify the problem, define their tasks, and plan computer activities. For example, such work sheets might prompt students to list key words for Internet searches, identify database field names and formats, find spreadsheet formulas, and create presentation storyboards and outlines.

Activities After Using the Computer. The "after-computer" activities are a critical component of the problem-solving process because it is in this step that students analyze the results of their research. One way to plan for this portion of the lesson is to create a "think sheet" of questions that guide students' learning. The questions should model an expert's approach to analyzing or interpreting the data. As students' cognitive skills develop, they can assist in developing think-sheet questions.

An after-computer sample think sheet related to the poet's garden might include the following two questions: What patterns emerged in relation to the type of flower and theme or time period of the poem? Which poets had favorite flowers, and how did these vary by country or time period? Similarly, a think sheet for students developing a menu for the long-distance runner might include the following analysis questions: What were the critical components of the weekly diet that could not vary from day to day? What was the most difficult part of the menu to maintain on a daily basis?

Supporting Activities. Most lessons will need some supporting activities beyond those completed on the computer, especially if computer access is limited. These activities might include readings, group discussions, lab, or field projects. Regardless of the nature of the supporting activities, professors must ensure that each activity supports achievement of the learning objectives.

Assessment. When using computers in a problem-based context, professors should consider using an alternative method of assessment in lieu of (or in combination with) traditional tests. Alternative assessments in problem-based activities are discussed in Chapter Eleven.

Guidelines for Using Computers as a Problem-Solving Tool

Professors who integrate computers as tools into problem-based lessons should realize that students may be learning two new instructional practices at once. After all, problem-based learning can occur without technology, and technology can be used in non-problem-solving contexts. However, professors who want to integrate computers as problem-solving tools into their courses can use the NTeQ model and the remaining articles from this volume as a foundation for modifying their instructional approach.

References

Green, K. C. "The 1999 National Survey of Information Technology in Higher Education: The Continuing Challenge of Instructional Integration and User Support." The Campus Computing Project, Oct. 1999. [http://www.campuscomputing.net]. Retrieved Aug. 1, 2001.

Ljung, E. J. "Finding Better Solutions with Problem-Based Learning." *Curriculum Update,* Summer 1997, pp. 5–6.

McEuen, S. F. "How Fluent with Information Technology Are Our Students?" *Educause Quarterly,* 2001, 24(4), 8–17.

Morrison, G. R., and Lowther, D. L. *Integrating Computer Technology into the Classroom.* (2nd ed.) Englewood Cliffs, N.J.: Merrill/Prentice Hall, 2002.

Rasmussen, K. "Using Real-Life Problems to Make Real-World Connections." *Curriculum Update,* Summer 1997, p. 8. [http://www.ascd.org/publications/curr_update/1997summer/rasmussen.html]. Retrieved July 11, 2003.

Rumbough, T. B. "Computer-Mediated Communication: Knowledge and Behaviors of Users." *College and University Media Review,* 1999, 5(2), 29–36.

DEBORAH L. LOWTHER *is associate professor of instructional design and technology at the University of Memphis.*

GARY R. MORRISON *is professor of instructional technology at Wayne State University, Detroit.*

5

To design is to solve problems. The author describes a model of problem solving through design that can be used to restructure courses, programs of study, or entire institutions.

Problem Solving Through Design

Wayne A. Nelson

Although problem-based learning (PBL) can be successful in individual classrooms, I am advocating a broader and more sweeping implementation of PBL that can extend across courses, degree programs, or even institutions. Specifically, I advocate the notion of PBL through design. In this article, I begin with a description of the relationship between design and problem solving. Next I offer an example of how I implemented "problem solving through design" across three graduate-level courses. Finally, I offer considerations for implementing a model of problem solving through design.

Connection Between Design and Problem Solving

Designing is a problem-solving process, and design problems are usually described as open-ended, unstructured, or "wicked" (Rittel, 1984). Whether designing something highly technical, like a computer-based flight simulator to train future pilots, or something far less technical, like a centerpiece flower arrangement for a formal table setting, we cannot design without inherently thinking and working in a problem-solving mode. Through both design and problem solving, we are focused on "changing existing situations into preferred ones" (Simon, 1996, p. 130).

Across disciplines, designers tend to share a common problem-solving process that is an open-ended analogue of the scientific method (Newell and Simon, 1972). Designers solve problems by employing a cyclical process of problem identification and analysis, research, and inquiry that leads to the ranking of design priorities, testing of multiple solutions through prototyping, and evaluating the design artifacts against performance criteria (Davis, 1998). To conceive this cyclical process in slightly different terms, we can note that design typically flows through four major stages: *naming* (identifying main issues in the problem), *framing* (establishing the limits of the problem), *moving* (taking an experimental design action), and *reflecting* (evaluating and criticizing the move and the frame). Schön (1991) notes that designers reflect on moves in three ways: by judging the desirability and consequences of the move, by examining the implications of a move in terms of conformity or violation of earlier moves, and by understanding new problems or potentials the move has created. Regardless of how we describe the process, the point is that designing, like problem solving, is based on systematic processes and situational "rules of thumb" (Perez, 1995) that should lead to purposeful and practical outcomes.

Example of Classroom That Uses Problem Solving Through Design

In a recent semester, I incorporated a problem-solving-through-design method into three graduate courses in instructional technology—an instructional design class, a software development class, and a project management class.

In the past, I had taught these courses using traditional approaches, including the use of in-class exercises based on decontextualized examples, readings from texts and journals, and final projects as a basis of evaluation. In these courses, collaboration was minimal. I recognized a huge limitation of this traditional approach. Because courses are removed from practical and authentic contexts, students come to see the content of courses as isolated stages of a process, not as integrated activities within a single process.

To "transform" these classes using a method of problem solving through design, I compiled several problem scenarios that included possibilities for real and simulated interaction with clients. I also designed a set of performance expectations that established major deadlines and described my ideas of various working relationships among the three classes. As I introduced the various problem scenarios to students at the beginning of the semester, I invited each class member to volunteer for problem scenarios that were personally appealing, although I monitored the process to ensure that at least one student from each class was on each design team. Once all students had volunteered for a team, I distributed the performance expectations document. Beyond adhering to the broad criteria in the performance expectations document, members of each team collaboratively worked to devise processes of design that would result in suitable artifacts.

Because each team was autonomous, no single description of the events that semester could fully capture each team's approach to design. In general, members of the project management class were in charge of the various projects. The project managers worked with the clients to establish project goals and tasks. Members of the design class assisted project managers in completing a needs assessment and analysis. Members of the design class also developed a design plan that members of the project management class presented to the client for approval. After the clients approved the various design plans, members of the software development class produced prototypes based on the plan created by the design class. The prototypes were tested with target audiences. The project management class then produced an evaluation report and held a culminating meeting with the design team to reflect on the process and outcomes of the design project.

Because students were enrolled in three different courses that met on three different nights, communication within each team was a potential problem. Project managers maintained Web sites for each problem scenario. These Web sites allowed all team members to view work schedules, drafts of design plans, and prototypes. Team members could communicate with each other and the client through e-mail. An important feature was that, using the Web sites as guides, each group, for the most part, was self-directed and self-sufficient.

I served as a consultant to the teams at various points of difficulty, as a "client" when quick decisions were necessary regarding project goals or vision, and as a team member when production problems arose. By the end of the semester, students had successfully completed seven projects, and students remarked that the process, while arduous, was also meaningful, fun, and afforded them opportunities to learn in ways that were different from those in traditional graduate classes.

Recommendations for Implementing Problem Solving Through Design

So far in this article, I have made a connection between design and problem solving. I also have described my attempts with implementing a problem-solving-through-design model across three higher education courses. In this section, I offer a vision of an environment that would fully support such a model. To implement a problem-solving-through-design approach, professors should reconceptualize curriculum as problems, place students in the role of designers, and reconfigure classrooms as design studios.

Curriculum as Problems. In a problem-solving-through-design model, professors cannot preestablish a curriculum. Even the idea of teaching design sensibilities as a topic in the curriculum is problematic because design is not an object of study; design is a mode of inquiry and exploration (Davis, Hawley, McMullan, and Spilka, 1997). Instead of a contrived curriculum presented through an artificial context, design tasks are supported by learning on demand, where learning goals emerge from the situation at hand. In other words, because design problems are ill structured, professors cannot determine a standard curriculum until students actively devise methods for addressing the design problem.

Although a predesigned curriculum is irrelevant in a problem-solving-through-design model, professors are necessary and vital to students' success. Professors serve as facilitators and share their expertise as experienced designers. Facilitators can help participants establish individual and small-group goals through the use of performance contracts (Rieber, 2000). The facilitator also can moderate evaluations, helping and encouraging learners to offer feedback to their peers. Most important, however, professors must serve as experienced designers by helping students formulate alternatives to solutions as students design.

Students as Designers. In a problem-solving-through-design model, students become designers. Designers work collaboratively and use conversation, argumentation, and persuasion to achieve consensus about perspectives and actions that might be taken to solve a design problem (Bucciarelli, 2001). Conflicting viewpoints are debated, and differences of opinion are negotiated. In this way, dialogue transforms individual thinking, creating collective thought and socially constructed knowledge within the team (Sherry and Myers, 1998). To further a shared understanding of the problem to be solved, designers create representations to solidify their design ideas (Hedberg and Sims, 2001).

Beyond working collaboratively, designers tend to be self-organized both individually and within their collaborative groups (Thomas and Harri-Augstein, 1985). Designers accept responsibility for their own learning by identifying their own purposes, setting goals for learning, implementing learning strategies, and identifying appropriate resources and tools (Fiedler, 1999).

Classrooms as Studios. To organize and manage design activities, professors can create an environment that is more akin to a studio than to a traditional classroom. Design studios are common in fine arts, architecture, and other fields that emphasize design (Orey, Rieber, King, and Matzko, 2000). Studios provide a learning environment in which participants use design tools and processes to complete real-world, and often self-selected, projects.

First, a design studio supports the use of appropriate design tools to craft models, drawings, narratives, and other representations of solutions. In many situations, professors may find that design activities provide excellent opportunities for the integration of computers into the classroom (for example, D'Ignazio, 1989; Liu and Pedersen, 1998). In other contexts, a consideration of communication tools can facilitate good design. As I note in my problem-solving-through-design example, students were officially registered for different courses, so a Web site became a valuable tool for promoting organization among students, and electronic communication tools became important tools for fostering clear communication.

Second, design studios support the use of processes that assist students in the design task. In general, students work independently and within teams to design a viable product that will solve their problem. For many students who have experience as designers, the idea of reflection may be natural and innate. But professors should consider building into the studio environment processes that will promote reflection among students. Professors need to scaffold reflection through concrete activities. For example, designers often maintain sketchbooks and diaries to support reflection (Cheng, 2000; Webster, 2001).

Also, professors can use numerous evaluation processes in design studios. They can conduct informal "desk critiques" on a regular basis. These desk critiques serve to provide students with cursory feedback about their work products. More formally, design studios imply the use of "juried" presentations of works in progress. In juried presentations, groups summarize their processes and showcase their products to professors and students who are working on other design projects. Juries provide an opportunity for formative peer review. In studios, summative evaluation often comes in the form of portfolios or formal presentations to faculty committees, other students, and possibly even real-world clients.

Conclusions

From students learning through the design and production of multimedia (Kahn and Taber Ullah, 1998) to students learning science by designing and testing solutions to problems (Harel and Papert, 1991), problem-solving-through-design tasks have become an effective model for teaching and learning. For students and professors, the use of design in the classroom presents new challenges and fundamentally alters their roles. In accepting the challenges of incorporating design into the classroom, professors create new learning experiences that are more appropriate for students, rather than relying on traditional exercises or lectures from a textbook.

References

Bucciarelli, L. "Design Knowing and Learning: A Socially Mediated Activity." In C. M. Eastman, W. M. McCracken, and W. C. Newstetter (eds.), *Design Knowing and Learning: Cognition in Design Education*. Amsterdam, N.Y.: Elsevier, 2001, pp. 297–314.

Cheng, N. "Web-Based Teamwork in Design Education." Paper presented at SiGraDi 2000: 4th Iberoamerican Congress of Digital Graphics, Rio de Janiero, Sept. 2000.

Davis, M. "Making a Case for Design-Based Learning." *Arts Education Policy Review,* 1998, *100*(2), 7–14.

Davis, M., Hawley, P., McMullan, B., and Spilka, G. *Design as a Catalyst for Learning.* Alexandria, Va.: Association for Supervision and Curriculum Development, 1997.

D'Ignazio, F. "The Multimedia Sandbox: Creating a Publishing Center for Students." *Classroom Computer Learning,* 1989, *10*(2), 22–23, 26–29.

Fiedler, S.H.D. "The Studio Experience: Challenges and Opportunities for Self-Organized Learning." Department of Instructional Technology, University of Georgia. [http://itech1.coe.uga.edu/studio/fiedler.html]. 1999.

Harel, I., and Papert, S. (eds.). *Constructionism.* Norwood, N.J.: Ablex, 1991.

Hedberg, J., and Sims, R. "Speculations on Design Team Interactions." *Journal of Interactive Learning Research,* 2001, *12*(2–3), 193–208.

Kahn, T. M., and Taber Ullah, L. N. *Learning by Design: Integrating Technology into the Curriculum Through Student Multimedia Design Projects.* Tucson: Zephyr Press, 1998.

Liu, M., and Pedersen, S. "The Effect of Being Hypermedia Designers on Elementary School Students' Motivation and Learning of Design Knowledge." *Journal of Interactive Learning Research,* 1998, 9(2), 155–182.

Newell, A., and Simon, H. A. *Human Problem Solving.* Englewood Cliffs, N.J.: Prentice Hall, 1972.

Orey, M., Rieber, L., King, J., and Matzko, M. "The Studio: Curriculum Reform in an Instructional Technology Graduate Program." Paper presented at the annual meeting of the American Educational Research Association, New Orleans, Apr. 2000.

Perez, R. "Instructional Design Expertise: A Cognitive Model of Design." *Instructional Science,* 1995, 23(5–6), 321–349.

Rieber, L. P. "The Studio Experience: Educational Reform in Instructional Technology." In D. G. Brown (ed.), *Best Practices in Computer Enhanced Teaching and Learning.* Winston-Salem, N.C.: Wake Forest Press, 2000, pp. 195–196.

Rittel, H. W. "Second-Generation Design Methods." In N. Cross (ed.), *Developments in Design Methodologies.* Chichester, U.K.: Wiley, 1984.

Schön, D. *The Reflective Practitioner: How Professionals Think in Action.* New York: Teachers College Press, 1991.

Sherry, L., and Myers, K. M. "The Dynamics of Collaborative Design." *IEEE [Institute of Electrical and Electronics Engineers] Transactions on Professional Communication,* 1998, *41*(2), 123–139.

Simon, H. A. *The Sciences of the Artificial.* (3rd ed.) Cambridge, Mass.: MIT Press, 1996.

Thomas, L., and Harri-Augstein, S. *Self-Organised Learning.* London, U.K.: Routledge, 1985.

Webster, H. "The Design Diary: Promoting Reflective Practice in the Design Studio." Paper presented at the Architectural Education Exchange, Cardiff, U.K., Sept. 2001.

WAYNE A. NELSON is professor of instructional technology and chair of the department of educational leadership at Southern Illinois University Edwardsville.

Professors who have never used problem-based learning (PBL) may need advice to support their first attempts. These professors can benefit from the confessions of one first-time (and initially reluctant) PBL user.

Problem-Based Learning in an MBA Economics Course: Confessions of a First-Time User

David C. Sharp

Economists generally perceive themselves as providers of rigor in business education (O'Rourke, 1998); admittedly, I am no exception. My methods of providing that rigor, however, continue to evolve. Like so many others trained in the neoclassical tradition, I entered the academy with notions of grandeur about the enterprise of teaching and learning economics. I, like many young academics, was ready to offer students the benefit of my theoretical and empirical wisdom. I, by virtue of my educational training and academic degrees, was ready to show students (in two-dimensional euclidian space) what they needed to know to be successful in the field of economics. Students would benefit so much from my insightful lectures!

Once in the academy, however, I was attacked by naysayers who were skeptical of my plans on *how* to contribute to the knowledge and skills of students. Instead of discussing the powerful insights of rigorous, relevant economic theory, they pontificated (on and on) about the virtues of the student-centered classroom, student exploration, collaboration, and process-based learning. And their scholarly literature characterized my role in the classroom with words that seemed endless and befuddling—coach (Kraft, 1988), tutor (Gijselaers, 1995), guide by the side (Stinson and Milter, 1996), facilitator (Anderson, Loviscek, and Webb, 2000), learning manager (Kirch and Carvalho, 1998), and project supervisor in the student-supervisor interface (Johnson and Snaith, 1998). Meanwhile, I had hoped only to be called "professor."

The rhetoric of these student-centered evangelists—mixed with the vehemence with which they assaulted my preconceived notions—prompted me to retaliate, although duplicitously. Although I initially described their methods as sounding "touchy feely" and "fluffy," their message was secretly sinking in. I began to question my techniques and came to realize that the "chalk-'n'-talk" model of instruction so pervasive in economics (Caropreso and Haggerty, 2000) did leave something to be desired. I decided to integrate problem-based learning (PBL) into my classroom.

The purpose of this chapter is to describe my experiences as I used PBL for the first time. I begin by describing the problem that I used; then I describe the pedagogy that I used to integrate the problem into the curriculum. Although I describe the introduction of PBL to a Master's of Business Administration (MBA) class, my experiences can be generalized to first-time users across disciplines. At the end of this article, I offer implications for other, perhaps reluctant, professors who may be considering taking the initial steps for integrating PBL into their classrooms.

My PBL Problem

One of the major difficulties I faced was coming up with an appropriate problem to use in the classroom. The literature provided more in the way of general guidelines (for example, the problem should be ill structured, open ended, challenging, not too narrow, and authentic, while encouraging students to work together) than it did in the way of practical examples. I found no handy compilation of tried, true, and purist-approved PBL problems in economics, so it was clear that I had to undertake the task of designing my own. The difficulties of this task seemed exacerbated by most of the PBL literature, which tended to emphasize how disastrous the professor's use of a poorly designed problem can be (for example, Gijselaers, 1996; Gijselaers and Schmidt, 1990). Indeed, PBL purists leave the impression that an improperly designed problem can send humanity's educational pursuits permanently back to the Stone Age. Understandably, I was hesitant to design my own. Nevertheless, I did.

My PBL problem is presented below, followed by brief comments on the problem's objectives, origins, and solutions.

> The new director of pricing and promotions for Doubleday and Company Publishing has hired your group as consultants. Best-selling author Stephen King writes hardback novels that are published by Doubleday. Doubleday's net earnings from Mr. King's books come in the form of profits from sales to distributors whereas Mr. King's earnings come in the form of royalties (in this case, 10 percent of sales), which are paid by Doubleday. Notably, a stipulation in Mr. King's contract gives his agent some bargaining power in determining the distribution price.

Using data from sales of Mr. King's previous books, Doubleday's econometricians have determined the demand curve for his new book: $Q = 50,000 - 500P$, where Q is the number of books and P is the price in dollars. Before the new director of pricing and promotions was hired, Doubleday's standard practice was to minimize costs—that is, produce and price hardbacks at the point where average total costs are minimized. Doubleday's director of production claims that manufacturing costs equal $2Q + 0.001Q^2$, plus $5,000 in fixed retooling overhead (all other fixed costs have been amortized).

Price negotiations with Mr. King's agent are scheduled for October 31, 2002. The new director of pricing and promotions is thoroughly confused. His job is to maximize profits for Doubleday. He wants your group to help him determine what price to charge for Mr. King's new hardback book.

Are there likely to be differences between Doubleday's standard price, the price the new director of pricing and promotions would like to set to maximize Doubleday's profits, and the price Mr. King's agent would like to set to optimize Mr. King's earnings? Determine and discuss the differences (if any) in price, output, and profit that will result from the standard Doubleday strategy, the new director's strategy, and the agent's strategy. What will you advise the new director of pricing and promotions to do? What are the advantages and disadvantages of your advice? Given everything we have learned about economic thinking, what (if anything) justifies your advice?

MBA curriculum typically emphasizes applications in the business world. With this emphasis in mind, my objective was to create a problem that reinforced the fact that various stakeholders (that is, the agent, the director, and the old regime) commonly have different incentives and strategies. Familiarity with these alternative incentives and strategies is important for informed decision making. And in this case, it may take a little calculus to fully appreciate these alternatives and to arrive at an informed decision.

This particular problem originated from various economic textbooks. I simply compiled ideas from various end-of-chapter questions and exercises that I gleaned from assorted economics texts, put the various ideas in a single context, and tried to couch that context with realistic-sounding names and plausible numerical values. I recognize that these origins may be controversial because end-of-chapter exercises often are narrowly focused on individual chapter topics and almost always have unique correct answers that are relatively easy to discern simply by reading the chapter. Because of the narrowness and simplistic nature of these exercises, many PBL theorists would completely and outrightly renounce their use. In the case of unaltered end-of-chapter exercises, such renouncements may be valid. However, I concur with Allen, Duch, and Groh (1996) that end-of-chapter exercises can serve as the foundation for a richer, more complex PBL problem with a scope that far transcends the original.

The solutions to the problem are of two different types. On the one hand, students can calculate *correct* values of price, output, and profit in alternative scenarios that the problem mentions (although approaches may differ substantially). On the other hand, the really big questions in this problem—"What will you advise the new director of pricing and promotions to do?"—do not have nice, tidy, unique, correct solutions.

According to the literature, PBL purists much prefer "ill-structured" problems containing multiple solutions that are, among other things, more indicative of what students will face in the real-world of work. When designing my problem, I completely understood this perspective. But in the end, I decided that an abrupt transition to pure PBL would be too radical of a departure for me to achieve in a semester. Furthermore, I felt that *some* well-structured components requiring correct answers would not completely destroy the mission of the problem. Finally, I thought that a mix of well- and ill-structured problems could help some students better make the transition from a classroom based on "right answers" to a new learning environment based on analyzing and solving real-world problems that often are ill structured and messy.

Implementation of the Problem into the Classroom

As I mentioned previously, I introduced the example problem to students enrolled in an MBA course. This particular course is an economics "bridging course," intended to provide students with economic fundamentals while maintaining a managerial character of applied practicality. Typically, fewer than fifteen students enroll in any one section of this course, and commonly about half of the students have engineering backgrounds. The size of the class and the diverse background of students made this an ideal course for me to begin experimenting with PBL as a pedagogical approach. I describe the process of implementing the problem into my class in three basic phases: an introductory phase, a discussion phase, and a presentation phase.

The introductory phase involved simply assigning students to groups and then distributing the PBL problem to the groups. Nine students were enrolled in my class; four students were engineers. I assigned groups such that each would have at least one engineer as a member. Given the mathematical nature of the problem and that I was not going to "spoon-feed" a mathematical approach for the students merely to parrot back to me, I wanted to ensure that each group had at least one member with a significant mathematical background. I hoped this distribution of students with strong math backgrounds would alleviate any terror felt by the slight majority of "math-phobes" in the class. (See Chapter Eight of this volume for more discussion about grouping students.)

I introduced the problem by providing a handout. In addition to the problem, the handout contained five simple ground rules:

Your group should meet at least once a week to discuss this problem and
work toward solutions.

You may use any printed resources necessary to arrive at solutions.

You may not consult with members of another group.

You may not consult me—or any other faculty member—outside of class
unless everyone in the group is confused.

As a group, you will submit typed solutions and present and explain your
results (or a portion of your results) six weeks from today during class.

In hindsight, these five simple rules seemed to work well in keeping
the groups organized and focused. Admittedly, however, I do not know
if they abided by these rules, and I did little to "police" their activity. My
intention was to simply get them working collaboratively to solve the
problem.

The discussion phase describes our regularly scheduled class times for
five weeks following the introductory phase. During these class sessions, we
discussed readings from the assigned principles of economics text.
Importantly, this text, as well as our discussions, contained issues relevant
to the PBL problem but fell short of providing solutions—or even mathematical approaches—for the objective portions of the problem. Specifically,
the class discussed such germane issues as revenue maximization (that
is, the agent's strategy), cost minimization (the old regime's strategy), and
profit maximization (the new director's strategy), but we never discussed
these topics in the context of the PBL problem.

Six weeks after I introduced the PBL problem, students presented and
explained a portion of their results during class. Specifically, because there
were three different price-output-profit combinations—that is, of the agent,
the director, and the old regime—and three class groups, each group presented a price-output-profit combination. Specifically, each group desig-
nated a presenter who then provided mathematical solutions for their given
combination. Following the presentation of these mathematical solutions,
each group shared its solutions to the more open-ended questions ("What
will you advise the new director of pricing and promotions to do? What are
the advantages and disadvantages of this decision? Given everything
we have learned about economic thinking, what, if anything, justifies this
decision?").

Implications

My notions of providing rigor in my classes have evolved. I have come to
understand the virtues of PBL and have been genuinely pleased by the
results. However, because it was not that long ago when I first introduced
PBL into my classroom, I remember well some of the difficulties associated
with the transition. From my experiences, I suggest the following to first-
time PBL users across the curriculum:

Some PBL Is Better Than None. It is not necessary to completely replace your current teaching methods in your first semester of PBL. I began with one PBL problem. My experience is in accord with that of Forsythe (2001); some PBL within the curriculum is better than none.

Keep the Ground Rules Simple. In my experience, ground rules need not be exhaustive or complex to keep the mission of the PBL problem, or the endeavors of the groups, organized and focused.

Create Your Own PBL Problems by Compiling and "Spicing Up" Ideas from Multiple Sources. You likely will discover the same dearth of handy PBL problem compilations in your discipline that I discovered in economics. You can design PBL problems by stringing together components of various exercises from multiple chapters (Allen, Duch, and Groh, 1996). Furthermore, a little inspiration from real-world sources (press, radio, or television) or discipline-specific literature (journal articles) can make the amalgam of end-of-chapter exercises more interesting and authentic.

Having *Some* "Right Answers" Does Not Make It Wrong. For the novice PBL professor, not to mention the nascent PBL student, some well-structured components of a problem that culminate in right answers may be useful and reassuring. Although some people may infer otherwise from PBL literature, the inclusion of some right answers need not be viewed as a high crime against humanity, especially when you are just starting out with PBL. Students may be so well ingrained in the traditional model of education that they are not able to tackle a completely open-ended, ill-structured problem that is devoid of any correct solutions.

References

Allen, D. E., Duch, B. J., and Groh, S. E. "The Power of Problem-Based Learning in Teaching Introductory Science Courses." In L. Wilkerson and W. H. Gijselaers (eds.), *Bringing Problem-Based Learning to Higher Education: Theory and Practice.* New Directions for Teaching and Learning, no. 68. San Francisco: Jossey-Bass, 1996, pp. 43–52.

Anderson, R. I., Loviscek, A. L., and Webb, J. R. "Problem-Based Learning in Real Estate Education." *Journal of Real Estate Practice and Education,* 2000, *3*(1), 35–41.

Caropreso, E. J., and Haggerty, M. "Teaching Economics." *College Teaching,* 2000, *48*(2), 69–75.

Forsythe, F. P. "Case Study: Using Problem Based Learning (PBL) to Teach Economics." Learning and Teaching Support Network, Institute for Learning and Research Technology, University of Bristol, 2001. [http://www.economics.ltsn.ac.uk/show-case/forsythe_pbl.htm].

Gijselaers, W. "Perspectives on Problem-Based Learning." In W. Gijselaers and others (eds.), *Educational Innovation in Economics and Business Administration: The Case of Problem-Based Learning.* Dordrecht, Netherlands: Kluwer, 1995, pp. 39–52.

Gijselaers, W. "Connecting Problem-Based Practices with Education Theory." In L. Wilkerson and W. H. Gijselaers (eds.), *Bringing Problem-Based Learning to Higher Education: Theory and Practice.* New Directions for Teaching and Learning, no. 68. San Francisco: Jossey-Bass, 1996, pp. 13–21.

Gijselaers, W., and Schmidt, H. G. "The Development and Evaluation of a Causal Model of Problem-Based Learning." In Z. Nooman, H. G. Schmidt, and E. Ezzat (eds.),

Innovation in Medical Education: An Evaluation of Its Present Status. New York: Springer, 1990, pp. 95–113.

Johnson, A., and Snaith, T. "Project-Based Learning in Leisure Management Training." In R. G. Milter, J. E. Stinson, and W. H. Gijselaers (eds.), *Educational Innovation in Economics and Business III.* Dordrecht, Netherlands: Kluwer, 1998, pp. 189–211.

Kirch, D. P., and Carvalho, G. "The Delivery of Accounting in the Problem-Based Learning Environment." In R. G. Milter, J. E. Stinson, and W. H. Gijselaers (eds.), *Educational Innovation in Economics and Business III.* Dordrecht, Netherlands: Kluwer, 1998, pp. 131–143.

Kraft, R. "Coaching to Learn." *Teaching Professor,* 1988, 2(1), 1–2.

O'Rourke, B. K. "Roles of Economics in Business and Management Education." In R. G. Milter, J. E. Stinson, and W. H. Gijselaers (eds.), *Educational Innovation in Economics and Business III.* Dordrecht, Netherlands: Kluwer, 1998, pp. 51–63.

Stinson, J. E., and Milter, R. G. "Problem-Based Leaning in Business Education: Curriculum Design and Implementation Issues." In L. Wilkerson and W. H. Gijselaers (eds.), *Bringing Problem-Based Learning to Higher Education: Theory and Practice.* San Francisco: Jossey-Bass, 1996, pp. 33–42.

DAVID C. SHARP is assistant professor of economics in the division of business and economic development at the University of Southern Mississippi Gulf Coast.

Heuristics often play a valuable role in solving problems. In this chapter, the author offers a problem-solving model that employs various general heuristics that may be tailored for specific applications across disciplines.

Heuristics and Problem Solving

Charles F. Abel

For many, "the central point of education is to teach people to think, to use their rational powers, [and] to become better problem solvers" (Gagné, 1985, p. 85). Toward this end, scholars have developed numerous problem-based teaching strategies and problem-solving models from a variety of theoretical frameworks. Many of the strategies and models indicate a significant role for heuristics.

I begin this chapter by defining *heuristics*. I then discuss their relevance in problem-solving frameworks. Finally, I present a heuristic model of problem solving that may be useful in promoting problem-solving skills across disciplines.

Heuristics and Problem Solving: Definitions, Benefits, and Limitations

The term *heuristic*, from the Greek, means, "serving to find out or discover" (Todd and Gigerenzer, 2000, p. 738). In the context of problem solving, heuristics are experientially derived cognitive "rules of thumb" that serve as guides in problem-solving processes. Heuristics guide problem solvers by helping them simplify choices regarding the numerous immensely complex and imperfectly understood factors that act simultaneously to shape problems.

Benefits of Heuristics in Problem Solving. As guidelines for problem solving, heuristics prove surprisingly robust across a wide array of problem types and problem contexts (Todd and Gigerenzer, 2000), proving remarkably accurate in both laboratories (Orbell and Dawes, 1991) and real-life contexts (Todd and Gigerenzer, 2000). Successful problem solving is a function of how efficiently, rather than how strenuously, a problem solver works (Anokhin and others, 1996), and heuristics enhance efficiency regardless of whether the problem is well structured (Anderson, 1993) or ill structured (Chi and Glaser, 1985). Some studies suggest that heuristic reasoning processes appear most useful in concrete situations (Todd and Gigerenzer, 2000). In fact, heuristics can help produce results that are comparable to problem-solving strategies that take into account all available information and employ complex computational processes (Todd and Gigerenzer, 2000; Heiner, 1983).

Limitations of Heuristics in Problem Solving. Heuristics do not guarantee correct solutions to problems (Mayer, 1983). Being based on generalized rules of thumb, heuristics may yield only approximate solutions. Also, effectively selecting and applying heuristics seem to require some conceptual and informational expertise (Wood, 1988). One type of misapplication commonly occurs when problem solvers use heuristics in situations where logic and probability theory would have been more effective (for example, Kahneman and Tversky, 1979).

Heuristics and Models of Problem Solving

Given the nature, function, and demonstrated efficacy of heuristics, it is not surprising to find them incorporated into many already-existing problem-solving models. Space limitations prevent me from elaborating on the numerous ways that various models employ heuristics, but the point of my examples below is to show that numerous problem-solving models from a variety of theoretical frameworks depend on heuristic reasoning for their success.

Some behaviorist models reduce problem solving to a simple heuristic—try options as they present themselves and systematically eliminate ineffective options. By way of contrast, gestalt models involve a three-step heuristic: Carefully analyze a problem domain to learn all that you can about that domain; find a different problem domain that is similar but more familiar and thus can be a "model"; and if you cannot find a similar domain, reformulate the problem (Wertheimer, 1945).

Probability models involve numerous heuristics that can provide direction to problem solvers. A simple cost-benefits analysis provides an example: When the costs of further problem solving outweigh the benefits, the problem is no longer worth solving (for example, Sargent, 1993; Stigler, 1961). Symbolic manipulation models also draw on heuristics for their efficiency. Problem solvers should draw a distinction between analytical problem solving and goal-directed problem solving, and heuristics can guide this distinction. Analytical problem solving is best achieved through the application of logical rules or the manipulation of mental models, both of which, in themselves, can be guided heuristically. The purpose of analytical problem solving is to find an optimal solution to problems. Realistically, though, successful problem-solving strategies seem to involve strategies that are generally reliable and efficient rather than "optimal" (Evans and Over, 1996). To pursue reliability, problem solvers often employ numerous heuristics to work through a problem and evaluate their incremental progress toward a reliable solution (Chase and Simon, 1973).

Inclusive Model of Heuristic Problem Solving

Based on the value of heuristics and their use in already-existing problem-solving models, I now offer a heuristic model of problem solving that may be useful for guiding students to solutions across disciplines. I recognize the difficulties of a general model designed to serve professors and students across disciplines. As Jonassen (1997) notes, problem solving is domain specific; therefore, a one-model-fits-all approach may be problematic.

Still, the model that I present in Figure 7.1 can heuristically serve as a frame for problem solving across disciplines. An important feature is that this frame is based on an analysis of already-existing problem-solving models that employ numerous discipline-specific heuristics. Within each level of the frame, I promote the use of heuristic questions as a means of prompting students' critical thinking while still simplifying choices.

Representation Heuristics. To begin solving a problem, students should create a concrete representation for that problem. By making the problem concrete, students can more easily "see" complicating issues that are often abstract. The irony is that although no one correct form of representation exists, problem solvers can improve performance when they strike upon the "right" representation (Kotovsky and Simon, 1990). Professors can guide students through representing the problem by using numerous heuristic questions:

What representation of the problem is most likely to provide a path toward a solution (Levin, Schneider, and Gaeth, 1998)?

Figure 7.1. A General Heuristic Model for Problem Solving

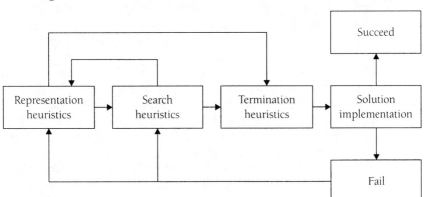

Do representations exist that accurately include all characteristics of the current problem while systematically excluding exogenous or irrelevant characteristics (Levin, Schneider, and Gaeth, 1998)?

Is there a way to represent this problem that you are most familiar and comfortable with (Todd and Gigerenzer, 2000)?

What are the discipline-specific norms for representing the problem?

This last heuristic question is particularly important for students to address. Professors should acknowledge the broad variety of possibilities for representing a problem—written documents, flow charts, diagrams, and three-dimensional models, for example—but students should understand discipline-specific norms. For instance, theologians and biologists are likely to use vastly different representations. By discussing discipline norms for representing problems, professors can help students see that they should represent problems in ways that are considered acceptable within a field of study (White, 1992) as a means of defining themselves as potential members of that field (Kuhn, 1970). Also, by helping students to consider differences in norms across disciplines, professors can expand students' ability to represent problems in increasingly flexible ways.

Search Heuristics.   Once students represent problems in meaningful ways, they should analyze the representations to identify functional and insightful elements within a problem. Numerous heuristic questions might be useful for guiding students toward determining salient elements:

What relationships and patterns among elements of the problem are evident in this representation (Kintsch and Greeno, 1985)?

Do any of the relationships or patterns evident within the representation seem to point to a solution (Kintsch and Greeno, 1985)?

Does any single element in the problem representation suggest a next step for solving the problem (Todd and Gigerenzer, 2000)?

Beyond using these heuristic questions as a guide, professors can help students take a more intuitive approach to analyzing the problem representation. For students who have some experience solving problems, simply asking them to determine similarities between the current problem representation and representations of previous problems that they are familiar with can prompt students' thinking toward possible important characteristics of the problem representation (Todd and Gigerenzer, 2000).

Termination Heuristics.   Ideally, based on the search heuristics, students will end up with one clear-cut choice for a potential solution. Therefore, termination heuristics will be unnecessary. But most problems are ill structured, so one clear-cut answer rarely surfaces. Professors should use the termination phase to help students see that not all problems culminate in single and clear solutions. In fact, professors can help students see that terminating a problem-solving activity is sometimes simply a matter of running out of time.

One termination heuristic is based on finding the answer that will suffice. This heuristic is helpful when a problem involves an unknown number of viable options. This heuristic requires students to consider two questions: What single criterion could serve as an aspiration level for a solution? and Have you found a potential solution that meets that criterion? Once students can answer the second question with a "yes," they are ready to implement the solution.

Implementation Heuristics. Superficially, an implementation heuristic is simply a matter of answering a question about the success of a solution: Is the implementation successful in solving the problem? Addressing this question can be complex, and numerous variables can contribute to this complexity. In helping students evaluate implementation, professors can help students simply determine a "yes" or "no" answer to the question of success. Should implementation fail, professors can guide students through reviewing their application of the problem-solving model in this article and reemploying the various heuristics within this model.

Conclusion

In this article, I have offered a problem-solving model based in heuristic thinking. Although this model is based on numerous already-existing problem-solving models, it employs several general heuristics that prove useful in a variety of contexts and across a wide range of subject domains. Thus, although simple in design, it allows professors to include domain-specific content and gear problem-solving processes toward the needs of a specific group of students.

References

Anderson, J. R. "Problem Solving and Learning." *American Psychologist,* 1993, *48,* 35–44.
Anokhin, A. P., and others. "Age Increases Brain Complexity." *Electroencephalography and Clinical Neurophysiology,* 1996, *99,* 63–68.
Chase, W. G., and Simon, H. A. "Perception in Chess." *Cognitive Psychology,* 1973, *4,* 55–81.
Chi, M.T.H., and Glaser, R. "Problem Solving Ability." In R. J. Steinberg (ed.), *Human Abilities: An Information Processing Approach.* New York: W.H. Freeman, 1985, pp. 227–250.
Evans, J., and Over, D. *Rationality and Reasoning.* Hove, U.K.: Psychology Press, 1996.
Gagné, E. *The Cognitive Psychology of School Learning.* Boston: Little, Brown, 1985.
Heiner, R. A. "The Origin of Predictable Behavior." *American Economic Review,* 1983, *73,* 560–595.
Jonassen, D. H. "Instructional Design Model for Well-Structured and Ill-Structured Problem-Solving Learning Outcomes." *Educational Technology Research and Development,* 1997, *45*(1), 65–95.
Kahneman, D., and Tversky, A. "Prospect Theory: An Analysis of Decisions Under Risk." *Econometrica,* 1979, *47*(2), 263–292.

Kintsch, W., and Greeno, J. G. "Understanding and Solving Word Arithmetic Problems." *Psychological Review,* 1985, *92,* 109–129.

Kotovsky, K., and Simon, H. A. "What Makes Some Problems Really Hard? Explorations in the Problem Space and Difficulty." *Cognitive Psychology,* 1990, *22,* 143–183.

Kuhn, T. S. *The Structure of Scientific Revolutions.* (2nd ed.) Chicago: University of Chicago Press, 1970.

Levin, I. P., Schneider, S. L., and Gaeth, G. J. "All Frames Are Not Created Equal: A Typology and Critical Analysis of Framing Effects." *Organizational Behavior and Human Decision Processes,* 1998, *76,* 149–188.

Mayer, R. *Thinking, Problem Solving, Cognition.* New York: Freeman, 1983.

Orbell, J., and Dawes, R. M. "A Cognitive Miser Theory of Cooperator Advantage." *American Political Science Review,* 1991, *85*(2), 515–528.

Sargent, T. J. *Bounded Rationality in Macroeconomics.* New York: Oxford University Press, 1993.

Stigler, G. J. "The Economics of Information." *Journal of Political Economy,* 1961, *69,* 213–225.

Todd, P. M., and Gigerenzer, G. "Précis of Simple Heuristics That Make Us Smart." *Behavioral and Brain Sciences,* 2000, *23,* 727–780.

Wertheimer, M. *Productive Thinking.* New York: Harper Collins, 1945.

White, H. *Identity and Control.* Princeton, N.J.: Princeton University Press, 1992.

Wood, D. J. *How Children Think and Learn: The Social Contexts of Cognitive Development.* Oxford, U.K.: Blackwell, 1988.

CHARLES F. ABEL is assistant professor in the department of political science at Stephen F. Austin State University, Nacogdoches, Texas.

To foster positive interaction among students in collaborative groups, professors can establish behavioral norms by the way they form groups and train students to work effectively in groups.

Fostering Collaboration Among Students in Problem-Based Learning

Bruce W. Speck

Problem-based learning (PBL), a pedagogical approach that uses complex scenarios or situations to engage students in seeking solutions to problems (Edens, 2000; Major and Palmer, 2001), is compatible with collaborative learning (Johnson, Johnson, and Smith, 1991; Stage, Muller, Kinzie, and Simmons, 1998). During collaborative learning projects, students work in groups to write a paper, construct a model, or produce some other product—all requiring problem-solving skills. However, because PBL and collaborative learning redefine the role of the professor and the students in the classroom, professors who want to link PBL with collaborative learning may seek advice about how to create and manage collaborative groups. In this chapter, I provide such advice by explaining how professors can form groups and train students to be successful collaborators.

Forming Groups

Collaborative groups can range in size from two to twelve, according to the literature on collaborative learning (for example, Bosley and Jacobs, 1992; Forman, 1989; Leverenz, 1994; Meyers, 1986), so there is no magic number that a professor can appeal to when determining how many students should be in a group. One factor for determining group size might be the complexity of the assignment and the extent of any written or oral product students are required to create. In some cases, the size of the group may be dictated by the need for sufficient laborers to complete the task given the time limitations of a semester.

New Directions for Teaching and Learning, no. 95, Fall 2003 © Wiley Periodicals, Inc.

Beyond group size, what other factors exist in forming groups? Professors might consider students' interest in a particular topic, personality types as identified by the Myers-Briggs Type Indicator (Collins, 1989; Jensen and DiTiberio, 1984; Spiegelhalder, 1983), compatibility of students' schedules for out-of-class meetings (Summers and Redmen, 1989), or age (Scheffler, 1992). In what follows, I focus on forming groups in light of concerns related to gender issues, cultural differences, and writing abilities.

Gender Issues. Concerning gender issues, opinion is divided about whether student groups should be homogeneous (Tebeaux, 1991) or gender balanced (Rehling, 1996). Lay (1992) and Sirc (1991) say that men and women have different communication styles, and literature on collaborative groups recognizes that gender differences can be the source of group difficulties, such as stereotyping women as secretaries and men as experts. Thus, women can become, de facto, secretaries for a group's work.

However, differences in communication styles between men and women can be a means of benefiting all members of a group (Atwood, 1992; Burnett and Ewald, 1994; Chiseri-Strater, 1991; Lay, 1989). Collaborative groups should be gender balanced because a primary purpose of education is to prepare students to work effectively in a variety of complex social situations, and few social situations in life are limited to a single gender. Indeed, to become effective lifelong problem solvers, students need to learn how to cope with communication styles based on gender.

Simply creating gender-balanced groups is not enough to prepare students for coping with diverse communication styles. Professors, therefore, may find it helpful to sensitize students to differences in the ways men and women communicate by asking students to respond to Markel's (1998) assertion that "women's communication patterns are more focused on maintaining the group, and men's on completing the task" (p. 62). Beginning a class discussion based on Markel's remark might help a professor to raise issues about respect for differences and the value of playing to another person's strengths.

In addition, professors can establish groups in which both genders have equal representation so that neither a man nor a woman is the odd person out. They might also intentionally call into question gender stereotypes by requiring that everyone in the group has the opportunity to assume a particular role that is associated with one gender, such as a secretary-in-rotation. In discussing gender roles, seeking to ensure balanced gender representation in groups, and challenging gender stereotypes, professors are sending a message to students that respect is a behavioral requirement for group life.

Cultural Differences. Cultural differences are another potential source of conflict when groups are formed. Unfortunately, professors may not be particularly sensitive to cultural differences (Speck, 1997). Thus, professors may need to examine their attitudes about nonnative students to ensure that those attitudes are not a hindrance to the behavioral requirement of respect in the classroom. (For professors interested in issues related to nonnative speakers' oral communication skills, I recommend Sigsbee, Speck, and Maylath's 1997 edited volume.)

In fact, professors may need to reexamine their cultural biases as a prelude to helping students probe their culture presuppositions. Consider, for instance, the educational ideal that students should learn how to effectively criticize other students' work. Such an ideal may be counter to a cultural ideal that a student is presumptuous in making negative comments (however true) about another student's work, especially when the student making the criticism is a nonnative speaker of English and the student being criticized is a native speaker (Allaei and Connor, 1990). Speck and Carmical (2002) describe a number of nonnative speakers' academic perspectives— for example, student-professor relationships, authority, classroom environment—that differ from typical American perceptions, so professors have a readily available source to consult about differing academic perspectives. As leaders of the classroom, professors have a distinct obligation to explore their perspectives on cultural differences to gain either a new or renewed appreciation of cultural diversity as a vital issue in PBL.

Professors can prepare students to work productively in PBL groups by providing students with readings on cultural differences and discussing those readings (Bosley, 1993). Students representing other cultures can explain to the class how American culture looks from a nonnative speaker's perspective. In addition, professors can invite other professors who represent other cultures to address the class about cultural differences. When a professor senses or sees that a nonnative speaker in a group is having difficulties of various sorts, the professor can seek a willing mentor from the group to help the struggling student. The efforts professors make to sensitize students to the value of cultural differences can help reinforce the message that cultural sensitivity is a behavioral requirement for classes.

Writing Abilities. Skills inherent to a problem-solving task can be valid criteria for grouping students. For example, students' abilities in using a statistical package, multimedia tools, or a scalpel may be valid reasons for determining groupings of students. Because writing is recognized as a premier way to promote student learning, many PBL groups will be asked to prepare written documents to demonstrate the depth of their learning.

Initially, professors may wonder whether student groups should be formed with writing skills as a criterion (Rothstein-Vandergriff and Gilson, 1988). If professors want to use writing skills as a criterion for sorting students into groups, they need to have a reliable way to determine students' writing abilities. Professors might, for instance, ask students to write one or more assignments before groups are formed to get some idea of students' writing abilities. Without any objective measure of students' writing skills, however, a professor's evaluation of students' writing is impressionistic. Although not devoid of merit, impressionistic evaluation is limited and can be fallible.

Often the argument for evaluating students' writing ability to assign students to groups is that strong and weak writers can be paired. The strong writers can help the weak writers, and the weak writers benefit from learning about good writing from the strong writers, so the argument goes. In reality, students who are good writers may usurp the opportunity for weak writers to learn more about writing because the strong writers take over the writing task to ensure that the weak writers will not unduly influence the group's grade. Perhaps, then, writing ability is not a useful criterion for establishing groups, especially if the goal of PBL groups is to "ensure that all members of a cooperative learning team feel a sense of responsibility for their teammates" (Cooper, Robinson, and McKinney, 1994, p. 75).

Training Students to Be Successful Collaborators

I have discussed issues related to forming groups from the perspective of introducing behavioral requirements that will promote effective collaboration during problem-based activities. Now I address other behavioral expectations related to leadership and conflict resolution.

Leadership. Professors should consider the need for effective leaders within student groups. However, they intentionally might decide not to select leaders but to allow leadership to arise naturally in a group. This approach requires the professor to monitor groups carefully so that natural leadership is effective. A professor can appoint formal group leaders using data about jobs students have had, leadership positions they have held in social organizations, parental responsibilities, desire for leadership, and so forth.

Another approach to selecting group leadership is to conceptualize the tasks a group must accomplish and assign a group member to a particular task. For instance, the professor could assign the role of scheduler to a group member, and the scheduler would ensure that the group adheres to its schedule, reporting to the professor periodically the group's success in subscribing to the schedule. The professor can ask the group to select a leader, but depending on the size of the school and the familiarity of students with each other, students may not have sufficient information to make an informed decision about who should lead the group. The professor can ask for volunteer leaders, but a danger in this approach is that a student may seek leadership to self-manage the group's work, even doing most of the work to ensure that the group performs according to the leader's best efforts. Whatever approach a professor uses to select group leaders, leadership must be monitored throughout a group project.

Conflict Resolution. According to Jehn (1997), task, relationship, and process are three types of intragroup conflict. Professors should establish group norms for dealing with those three types of conflict. For instance, they can clearly outline what a problem-based assignment entails to help students avoid task conflict. (For information on how to construct effective writing assignments, see Speck, 2000.) Professors can also establish procedures that groups can use to distribute work equitably to avoid task conflict—who does what.

To prepare students to deal with relationship conflict, a professor can inform students that negative attitudes and feelings about a group member are not permissible in the group. Thus, group members are required to act professionally. The professor can also announce that politeness and reasoned discourse are norms. Thus, all viewpoints are treated with respect. Disagreements are not to include name calling, ridicule, sexist remarks, or ethnic slurs. In short, as the leader in the classroom, the professor can establish behavioral norms that promote effective collaboration when students are engaged in PBL.

Conclusion

At times, literature on collaborative learning might seem to suggest that a focus on student learning requires the dismissal of professorial authority. I hope this article suggests that nothing could be further from the truth. Rather, for classrooms based on learner-centered models (like PBL) to be successful, professors must structure the classroom in ways that enable students to be effective collaborators.

The brief remarks in this chapter are suggestive of professors' role in creating effective collaboration among students, so professors may want to consult Speck (2002) for elaboration of the concepts presented here. Nevertheless, this chapter provides a framework for making decisions about how to form groups and train students to be effective collaborators when they are engaged in PBL.

References

Allaei, S. K., and Connor, U. M. "Exploring the Dynamics of Cross-Cultural Collaboration in Writing Classrooms." *Writing Instructor,* 1990, *10*(1), 19–28.

Atwood, J. W. "Collaborative Writing: The 'Other' Game in Town." *Writing Instructor,* 1992, *12*(1), 13–26.

Bosley, D. S. "Cross-Cultural Collaboration: Whose Culture Is It, Anyway?" *Technical Communication Quarterly,* 1993, *2*(1), 51–62.

Bosley, D. S., and Jacobs, J. "Collaborative Writing: A Philosopher's Guide." *Teaching Philosophy,* 1992, *15*(1), 17–32.

Burnett, R. E., and Ewald, H. R. "Rabbit Trails, Ephemera, and Other Stories: Feminist Methodology and Collaborative Research." *Journal of Advanced Composition,* 1994, *14*(1), 21–51.

Chiseri-Strater, E. *Academic Literacies: The Public and Private Discourse of University Students.* Portsmouth, N.H.: Boynton/Cook, 1991.

Collins, V. T. "Personality Type and Collaborative Writing." In R. Louth and A. M. Scott (eds.), *Collaborative Technical Writing: Theory and Practice.* Hammond, La.: Association of Teachers of Technical Writing, 1989, pp. 111–116.

Cooper, J. L., Robinson, P., and McKinney, M. "Cooperative Learning in the Classroom." In D. F. Halpern and Associates (eds.), *Changing College Classrooms: New Teaching and Learning Strategies for an Increasingly Complex World.* San Francisco: Jossey-Bass, 1994, pp. 74–92.

Edens, K. M. "Preparing Problem Solvers for the 21st Century Through Problem-Based Learning." *College Teaching,* 2000, *48*(2), 55–60.

Forman, J. "The Discourse Communities and Group Writing Practices of Management Students." In C. B. Matalene (ed.), *Worlds of Writing: Teaching and Learning in Discourse Communities of Work.* New York: Random House, 1989, pp. 247–254.

Jehn, K. A. "A Qualitative Analysis of Conflict Types and Dimensions in Organizational Groups." *Administrative Science Quarterly,* 1997, *42,* 530–557.

Jensen, G. H., and DiTiberio, J. K. "Personality and Individual Writing Processes." *College Composition and Communication,* 1984, *35*(3), 285–300.

Johnson, D. W., Johnson, R. T., and Smith, K. A. *Cooperative Learning: Increasing College Faculty Instructional Productivity.* ASHE-ERIC Higher Education Report, vol. 20, no. 4. Washington, D.C.: Graduate School of Education and Human Development, George Washington University, 1991.

Lay, M. M. "Interpersonal Conflict in Collaborative Writing: What We Can Learn from Gender Studies." *Journal of Business and Technical Communication,* 1989, *3*(2), 5–28.

Lay, M. M. "The Androgynous Collaborator: The Impact of Gender Studies on Collaboration." In J. Forman (ed.), *New Visions of Collaborative Writing.* Portsmouth, N.H.: Boynton/Cook, 1992, pp. 82–104.

Leverenz, C. S. "Peer Response in the Multicultural Composition Classroom: Dissensus—A Dream (Deferred)." *Journal of Advanced Composition,* 1994, *14*(1), 167–186.

Major, C. H., and Palmer, B. "Assessing the Effectiveness of Problem-Based Learning in Higher Education: Lessons from the Literature." *Academic Exchange Quarterly,* 2001, *5*(1), 4–8.

Markel, M. *Technical Communication: Situations and Strategies.* (5th ed.) New York: St. Martin's Press, 1998.

Meyers, G. D. "The Writing Seminar: Broadening Peer Collaboration in Freshman English." *Writing Instructor,* 1986, *6*(1), 48–56.

Rehling, L. "Writing Together: Gender's Effect on Collaboration." *Journal of Technical Writing and Communication,* 1996, *26*(2), 163–176.

Rothstein-Vandergriff, J., and Gilson, J. T. "Collaboration with Basic Writers in the Composition Classroom." Paper presented at the annual meeting of the Conference on College Composition and Communication, St. Louis, 1988. (ED 294 220)

Scheffler, J. A. "Using Collaborative Writing Groups to Teach Analysis of an RFP." *Bulletin of the Association for Business Communication,* 1992, *55*(2), 26–28.

Sigsbee, D. L., Speck, B. W., and Maylath, B. (eds.). *Approaches to Teaching Non-Native English Speakers Across the Curriculum.* New Directions for Teaching and Learning, no. 70. San Francisco: Jossey-Bass, 1997.

Sirc, G. "One of the Things at Stake in the Peer-Group Conference: The Feminine." Paper presented at the annual meeting of the Conference on College Composition and Communication, Boston, 1991. (ED 332 187)

Speck, B. W. "Respect for Religious Differences: The Case of Muslim Students." In D. L. Sigsbee, B. W. Speck, and B. Maylath (eds.), *Approaches to Teaching Non-Native English Speakers Across the Curriculum.* New Directions for Teaching and Learning, no. 70. San Francisco: Jossey-Bass, 1997, pp. 39–46.

Speck, B. W. *Grading Students' Classroom Writing: Issues and Strategies.* ASHE-ERIC Higher Education Report, vol. 27, no. 3. Washington, D.C.: Graduate School of Education and Human Development, George Washington University, 2000.

Speck, B. W. *Facilitating Students' Collaborative Writing.* ASHE-ERIC Higher Education Report, vol. 28, no. 6. San Francisco: Jossey-Bass, 2002.

Speck, B. W., and Carmical, B. H. (eds.). *Internationalizing Higher Education: Building Vital Programs on Campuses.* New Directions for Higher Education, no. 117. San Francisco: Jossey-Bass, 2002.

Spiegelhalder, G. "From Darkness into Light: A Group Process Approach to the Paper." *Arizona English Bulletin,* 1983, 26(1), 91–106.

Stage, F. K., Muller, P. A., Kinzie, J., and Simmons, A. *Creating Learning Centered Classrooms: What Does Learning Theory Have to Say?* ASHE-ERIC Higher Education Report, vol. 26, no. 4. Washington, D.C.: Graduate School of Education and Human Development, George Washington University, 1998.

Summers, T. F., and Redmen, D. L. "Problems Encountered While Group Writing: The Students' Point of View." In R. Louth and A. M. Scott (eds.), *Collaborative Technical Writing: Theory and Practice.* Hammond, La.: Association of Teachers of Technical Writing, 1989, pp. 95–100.

Tebeaux, E. "The Shared-Document Collaborative Case Response: Teaching and Research Implications of an In-House Teaching Strategy." In M. M. Lay and W. M. Karis (eds.), *Collaborative Writing in Industry: Investigations in Theory and Practice.* Amityville, N.Y.: Baywood, 1991, pp. 124–145.

BRUCE W. SPECK is professor of English and vice president for academic affairs at Austin Peay State University in Clarksville, Tennessee.

Professors who supervise students in field experiences have a unique challenge in helping students solve the problems that they face. The authors offer strategies for helping students analyze and solve problems that they experience in field experiences.

Guiding Students Toward Solutions in Field Experiences

Julia Beckett, Nancy K. Grant

Many universities provide students with the opportunity to participate in field experiences. For example, law students often serve as clerks for law firms or judges. Students in colleges of business often serve as interns for local corporations. In many disciplines, students must participate in field experiences to gain certification or to complete degree requirements. For example, education students who want to earn certification must student-teach under the guidance of a mentor teacher. Similarly, students in nursing, social work, and clinical psychology must participate in clinical work and field-based practicums.

Through these field experiences, students can make the transition from the college classroom to the world of work; yet, they still can benefit from the mentorship, supervision, and guidance of professors. In this chapter, we provide insight into how professors can achieve the difficult task of guiding students to solutions in field experience problems. We begin by offering strategies for helping students understand and solve problems in field experiences. We then use vignettes as a means of applying those strategies.

Strategies for Helping Students Analyze and Solve Problems

In field experiences, students encounter problems that are ill structured. Because one goal of field experiences is to prepare students for the workforce, which includes ill-structured problems, supervising professors should not solve the problem for students; rather, supervising professors should have a repertoire of strategies for helping students in the field understand and analyze problems. In this section, we offer suggested strategies that professors can use with individuals or with groups. Each of these strategies promotes Schön's (1987) view of promoting reflection among practitioners.

Reconnecting Practice to Theory. In traditional classrooms, professors are often in the position of helping students connect textbook readings to the real world. For professors who are supervising students engaged in field experiences, the challenge comes in helping students reconnect their practical experience to classroom theory. How can professors accomplish this goal?

One strategy is to have students review textbooks and other readings from courses. Example cases in texts and their corresponding explanations, for example, are suggestive and may be useful tools for helping students think about real-world problems in theoretical terms (Lynn, 1999; Barnes, Christensen, and Hanson, 1994). When students have the opportunity to reframe their practical problems in theoretical terms, they may be able to see their problems in new ways that were not previously evident.

Journal Keeping. Journal writing and other informal types of writing can help students analyze problems. In this respect, writing can become a way of knowing for students. Journal keeping involves documenting events within a field experience. Furthermore, journal keeping provides opportunities for students to respond to these events by elaborating on them and brainstorming questions about the events. Such elaboration and brainstorming can promote reflection among students, through which they gain a clearer perspective on problems and possible solutions.

Other types of informal writings might be useful to students, as well. For example, if professors are supervising many students in field experiences, they might consider establishing an electronic bulletin board for online discussion among students. Through participating in online discussion, students have the opportunity to share their field-experience problems and receive feedback from others who may have experienced similar problems. By using such an interactive approach, professors are providing students not only a forum for dealing with field-based problems but also an opportunity to build a sense of camaraderie based on their field experiences.

Role Playing. Role playing can be a powerful tool for analyzing interpersonal problems and developing strategies for solving those problems. When students role play a difficult conversation, for example, they may be more prepared to have the actual conversation. Moreover, taking on a new role might be helpful in analyzing a problem. For example, by having students play the role of a supervisor or coworker, professors can help students shift their perspective as they consider a problem.

Important to the success of role playing is the notion of "fish-bowl exercises," where students who watch the role-play scenario critique what they observe. Professors and students collaboratively can analyze the critiques, which will generate further conversation about the problem and potential solutions inherent to the role-play scenario. Based on these critiques and analyses, students can role play the scenario again to incorporate some of the suggestions and ideas of the group.

Socratic Conversations. Simple one-on-one conversations between a professor and a student who encountered a problem in a field experience can be useful. We are not suggesting that these conversations should be an opportunity for supervising professors to berate (or even lecture) students about mistakes they may have made in the field. In fact, although professors may have preconceived notions about the type of conversation that will be most useful to a student experiencing a problem, professors should analytically but conversationally guide students through an analysis of their experiences and the problems that they encounter by asking open-ended questions and encouraging students to elaborate: "tell me more about that." In what follows, we describe two analytical approaches that might be useful in guiding students during conversations.

First, situation analysis is a tool to guide students through the process of explaining the details of a problem situation. By asking open-ended questions, professors can determine events leading up to a problem, complications to an already-existing problem, and contributing factors that may sustain or alleviate the problem. Situation analysis provides students an opportunity to articulate the problem to an interested audience. This process of articulation helps them overcome any knee-jerk reactions to the problem and think about it in more analytical terms.

Second, sometimes students need to consider their problem from a larger perspective. An organizational analysis can help students acknowledge (or realize) the purpose of an organization and how their role in the organization contributes to that purpose. In metaphorical terms, an organizational analysis can help students see that they (and the problems they encounter) are one tree in a much larger forest. As professors engage students in discussing the organization in which they are interning, students come to see their problem in light of larger institutional factors.

Applying the Strategies

In the previous section, we offered numerous strategies that professors can use to help students analyze, and thus begin to solve, problems that they encounter in field experiences. In this section, we offer vignettes of students who are experiencing problems in their field experiences. After each vignette, we apply strategies from the previous section to show how professors might use these strategies in conjunction with each other to help students solve problems.

Vignette One: Dissatisfied Students. As the following example shows, students are sometimes unhappy with the realities of their role in a field experience:

> Irma, a local government intern, tells Professor Nash that her internship is
> not what she expected. The work seems menial. She is only responding to
> inquiries for information about the agency's regulations and procedures. She
> concludes her explanations by saying to Professor Nash, "I don't see how this
> is preparing me for a career in management."

The professor sympathizes with Irma and even secretly wishes that the
agency hosting Irma's internship would use interns for more than sending
information about the agency and fielding cursory phone calls. Nevertheless, the professor must deal with the realities of the field experience and
the student's concerns.

The professor guides the conversation toward helping Irma recognize
the importance of her job in light of larger questions about the purpose
of the organization in which she works: Who is requesting information
about the agency's regulations and procedures? What happens if those
inquiring about procedures do not follow them correctly? Is disseminating
the information to inquiries important in light of the agency's overall mission and function?

Although the conversation helps the student begin to understand the
relationship between her job and the agency's larger goals, the professor recognizes that part of the student's concern deals with the skills that she is
gaining in the internship. To address this issue, the professor suggests a
future conversation about the student's field experience but asks her to
spend some time looking back at her management textbooks from courses
that she has taken. Specifically, the professor suggests that she spend some
time finding characteristics of effective managers and making a list of how
her internship is helping her develop these characteristics. Based on what
the student discovers (or fails to discover) about the connection between
her field experience and the characteristics of a good manager, the professor can continue the conversation with her.

Vignette Two: Ethical Dilemmas. A different sort of problem occurs
when students raise questions about unethical behavior:

> Ronald tells Professor Fiske his concerns about possible improprieties in the
> accounting department of the large hotel where he is interning. One of
> Ronald's responsibilities is to compile a weekly report for senior management.
> This report details the number of rooms sold and room rates. Yet, Ronald's
> manager insists that Ronald adjust room rates to show a standard price, not
> an actual one. In other words, Ronald's report does not reflect discount rates
> that might have been given as incentive to large groups or as appeasement to
> angry hotel guests. These adjustments do not change the bottom-line figures
> on the report, but they do change line items on the report from actual room
> rates to "standard" room rates. Ronald's manager told Roger that these adjust-
> ments will simply be clearer for senior management. Ronald notes, "A senior
> manager has called an accounting department meeting for next week, and I
> know the accuracy of the reports will be an issue."

The professor listens carefully and determines that the situation is unusual but only possibly unethical. As coordinator of interns for her university's business school, the professor has established an electronic bulletin board dedicated to discussing field experiences. Also, she facilitates a weekly face-to-face seminar that students in field experiences attend. She suggests that the student describe his dilemma and concerns in the electronic bulletin board as a means of soliciting help from other students who are participating in various field experiences. In addition, the professor suggests that the student record ideas and reactions from his classmates and present them at the next seminar meeting.

The professor also suggests that at the next seminar, she will facilitate some role plays about this situation. These role plays will provide the student an opportunity to practice a discussion with the manager about the hotel's accounting practices. The role plays also will allow Ronald to experience various scenarios that could emerge in the accounting meeting that was scheduled for the next week.

Vignette Three: Performance Problems. Sometimes interns have difficulty performing their assigned jobs. Consider the following example:

> Marie is a civil engineering student who is interning with a county transportation department. She tells Professor Percept that she was given the task of prioritizing intersections that are most in need of traffic lights or stop signs. Marie notes that she easily was able to establish a method and to calculate traffic patterns. However, she is at a loss on reporting her findings. "I've never written a report of this magnitude," she notes. "And I've never had to defend my recommendations so thoroughly and formally." Marie expresses concern about approaching her supervisor for fear of seeming incompetent.

After listening to the student's concerns, the professor determines that the student is simply not confident in her abilities because of the real-world implications of her recommendations. Because of the professor's familiarity with the program of studies that prepared the student for her field experience, he suggests that she review notes and textbooks from previous courses. To help the student focus on salient issues of report writing and making recommendations, he even refers to specific courses and textbooks that might be useful for her to review.

In addition, the professor guides a conversation with the student about her relationship with her supervisor. The student describes her supervisor as firm and aggressive. As a result of this conversation, the professor determines that the student needs practice asking her manager for help. Using role playing during a field-experience seminar, the professor provides the student with practice; he also asks her to play the role of the supervisor in one role play. By taking on a new role, the student is likely to better understand her supervisor's perspectives. Practice boosts her confidence and thus her potential for successfully communicating with her supervisor.

Implications and Conclusions

Field experiences are designed to prepare students for the world of work, and as discussed in Chapter One of this volume, students will not be successful in the world of work unless they can analyze and solve problems. In this article, we have suggested strategies that professors can use as an entry point for helping students analyze and solve problems that they encounter in field experiences. Because our vignettes have been merely examples of possibilities for applying these strategies, we offer the following concluding perspectives and advice:

Helping students solve problems is more of an act of facilitation than of direct teaching. When professors lecture, students may feel dehumanized. When professors facilitate students' own active engagement in problem solving, students feel empowered.

Implementing our strategies initially may seem to foster more dependence on professors. We contend that through collaborative activities—like role play and bulletin-board discussions—students can help each other analyze and solve problems, which decreases dependence on professors.

In applying the strategies, professors can help students to focus on changing their own attitudes, thoughts, and behaviors. Often the problem is not inherent to the internship; rather, it may reflect the students' current understandings of the internship. Our strategies can help students adjust their own thinking and ideas.

References

Barnes, L. B., Christensen, C. R., and Hanson, A. J. (eds.). *Teaching and the Case Method: Text, Cases, and Reading.*, (3rd ed.) Boston: Harvard Business School Press, 1994.

Lynn, L. E. *Teaching and Learning with Cases: A Guidebook.* New York: Chatham House, 1999.

Schön, D. A. *Educating the Reflective Practitioner: Toward a New Design for Teaching and Learning in the Professions.* San Francisco: Jossey-Bass, 1987.

JULIA BECKETT *is assistant professor of public administration and urban studies at the University of Akron.*

NANCY K. GRANT *is professor of public administration and urban studies at the University of Akron.*

10

To promote metacognitive thinking, professors can help students articulate their motives and decisions during problem-solving activities.

Not All Metacognition Is Created Equal

Douglas J. Hacker, John Dunlosky

Metacognition is generally defined as knowledge that people have about thought processes and individual monitoring and control of their own thoughts (Hacker, 1998). In recent years, professors have encouraged students across disciplines to think about their problem solving by actively monitoring and controlling their own thinking. Although this approach can be valuable, some professors have unquestioningly adopted the belief that students who do "something" metacognitive will become better problem solvers.

Unfortunately, many advocates of metacognition have not recognized that, like most thought processes, metacognition is neither easily characterized nor easily stimulated in students, much less easily used as a psychological tool to promote problem solving (Kozulin, 1998). Moreover, merely promoting metacognition does not ensure its efficacy. For example, monitoring is commonly viewed as reflecting, but reflection is not always accurate and may even produce distorted views of one's thoughts (Nisbett and Wilson, 1977). Thus, before considering the use of metacognition as a learning strategy, professors must be aware of the characteristics and processes of metacognition. In this article, we offer a cursory framework of metacognition that illustrates its complexity, and then we describe some implications of this framework for improving students' problem solving.

Framework of Metacognition

Our major thesis (as well as the title of this article) is that not all metacognition is created equal. Because metacognition involves higher-level thoughts that "oversee" lower-level thoughts, the nature of metacognition depends on just *what* lower-level thoughts are being overseen and *how* those thoughts are being overseen. As the "what" and "how" vary, the effects of metacognition on problem-solving processes vary. Because we are interested in classroom applications, we elaborate on inequalities among metacognitive variations by focusing this article only on forms of metacognition that can be verbalized between professor and student. We first briefly introduce three types of verbal report and then distinguish between three levels of verbalization that can influence those reports. We argue that although each form of verbalization can be influential, one in particular will yield the most significant gains in problem solving.

Types of Verbal Report. Researchers interested in metacognition have made extensive use of three types of verbal report: concurrent, retrospective, and prospective (Table 10.1). Concurrent reports involve saying out loud whatever students are currently thinking. Retrospective reports reflect thoughts that students retrieve from past experiences. These reports are always descriptions of prior thinking and hence are more likely to be incomplete and subject to biases (Nisbett and Wilson, 1977). Last, prospective reports involve predicting future states of knowledge or predicting future performance on a task, such as an examination or problem-solving activity.

Levels of Verbalization. Ericsson and Simon (1980) identified three levels of verbalization (see Table 10.1). Although they identified these levels as finer distinctions of concurrent and retrospective reports, they also have analogues for prospective reports. Level 1 verbalizations involve simply reporting current verbal contents. Students need not expend any additional effort to verbalize these thoughts because they are already in a verbal form. Level 2 verbalizations involve reporting thoughts that are not in a verbal form (for example, talking about what one is doing while solving a Rubik's Cube). This kind of verbalization requires additional thinking as students recode nonverbal information into a verbal form.

Neither level 1 nor level 2 concurrent verbalizations likely change students' thought processes, and in studies that used these kinds of verbalizations, they neither helped nor hindered problem solving (Ericsson and Simon, 1993). Levels 1 and 2 retrospective and prospective verbalizations are metacognitive in nature. The types of verbalization illustrated in these four cells of Table 10.1 require that people monitor their thoughts and choose words to accurately verbalize them, either to characterize past thoughts (retrospective) or to develop a prediction of future performance on tasks (prospective). But like levels 1 and 2 concurrent verbalizations, the utility of these types of report for problem solving is uncertain.

Verbalizations That Promote Problem Solving. Level 3 verbalizations involve explaining the thoughts currently active in memory. Although we suspect that level 3 verbalization across all three types of verbal report has utility for problem solving, the empirical base supporting such a claim is minimal for retrospective and prospective reports. By contrast, the research base supporting the use of level 3 concurrent verbalizations as a

Table 10.1. Types of Verbal Reports and Levels of Verbalization

	Levels of Verbalization		
Types of Verbal Reports	Level 1 Verbalization of verbal contents	Level 2 Verbalization of nonverbal contents	Level 3 Verbalization of verbal or nonverbal contents that involves explaining those contents
Concurrent Reporting information as it forms concurrently with ongoing thinking	Reflects information that is currently in a verbal form Example: "Keep talking about what you're thinking as you read the story"	Reflects information that is currently in a nonverbal form and recoded into a verbal form Example: "Talk aloud as you work the Rubik's Cube"	Reflects information that is currently in a verbal or nonverbal form *and* the additional thinking that is potentially contributing to that information Example: "Explain how you make use of the rhetorical structures of the story as you read"
Retrospective Reporting from past experiences	Reflects verbal information that is being remembered from past experiences Example: "Tell me what you can remember about the story you read"	Reflects nonverbal information that is being remembered from past experiences and recoded into a verbal form Example: "What can you remember about how you worked the Rubik's Cube?"	Reflects verbal or nonverbal information that is being remembered from past experiences *and* the additional processing that information has undergone as a consequence of the retrieval process Example: "Now that you have read each story, explain how you comprehended the texts"
Prospective Reporting of current thoughts or remembered past experiences for the purpose of predicting future states	Reflects the verbal information that is being inferred from past experiences Example: "Now that you have read the story, how confident are you that you can correctly answer questions about it?"	Reflects the nonverbal information that is being inferred from past experiences and recoded into a verbal form Example: "Now that you have seen the first five moves of the Rubik's Cube, how confident are you that you can successfully complete it?"	Reflects the verbal or nonverbal information that is being inferred from past experiences *and* the additional thinking that underlies the inferential processing Example: "Explain how you could more accurately predict what you will remember about the story you just read when you are tested on it next week"

metacognitive strategy for promoting problem solving is strong (for a review, see Ericsson and Simon, 1993).

Level 3 concurrent verbalization requires students to explain their ongoing problem solving, give justifications for it, and to rationalize it as they are actively engaged. Hence, such verbalization promotes metacognitive thinking that can lead to more effective problem solving (Dominowski, 1998). Instructions that promote level 3 concurrent verbalization (for example, "Explain how you make use of the rhetorical structures of the story as you read") force students to go beyond simply reporting what they are thinking. They must deliberately change the course and structure of their thoughts as they verbalize responses to the instructions. Moreover, because such instructions can be conversational, students must think more to create a coherent response for listeners. This additional thinking may contribute to the benefits of level 3 concurrent verbalizations for problem solving (Dominowski, 1998).

Using Level 3 Concurrent Verbalizations in the Classroom

A professor's primary goal in using level 3 concurrent verbalizations during problem solving is to encourage students to verbalize their motives and reasons for what they are thinking while problem solving. Instructing students to explain how their thinking is being generated, how they know certain information, why a decision was made, or why they rejected a solution stimulates the kind of level 3 concurrent verbalization that is characteristic of the problem solving associated with expert performance (Dominowski, 1998). We call these instructions to verbalize "metacognitive probing." Professors' metacognitive probes should be tailored to the specific problem being solved and to the specific student and where that student is in the problem-solution process. Thus, level 3 concurrent verbalization may have its greatest utility when professors are working individually with students. However, this kind of verbalization can also be used with groups of students. As we illustrate the use of metacognitive probes with individual students and with groups, we focus on the problem solving required to accomplish an ill-structured task that is common in classrooms—writing a persuasive essay.

Instructing Individual Students. Professors should start by assessing a student's current understanding of the problem. Simple prompts will do: "Tell me what you know about writing a persuasive essay," or "Explain to me what you know about the process of persuading someone to your viewpoint." Possibly the student knows little about the problem, and his or her reports will help the professor stimulate level 3 concurrent verbalizations to guide students through the problem-solving process.

Once a student's background knowledge has been assessed, the professor can begin to use probes to stimulate level 3 concurrent verbalizations. A goal throughout this interaction is to ask simple questions that will help the student to explain his or her ongoing problem-solving activity. To get the student focused on initiating the problem-solving process, the professor can ask, "How are you beginning to solve the writing task?" or "What planning or writing strategy are you starting with?" The professor should ensure that the student is responding to these probes by verbalizing his or her thoughts. If the student is silent for more than fifteen seconds, the professor should pose additional probes such as, "What is the process in which you are engaged?" or "How are you deciding what should be written?" Long silences can indicate that the student is not yet adept at the verbalization procedure or is not actively thinking about the problem.

When students are blocked, professors can use additional probes: "What seems to be the difficulty?" or "What seems to be the main obstacle holding up your writing?" Or, if students fail to make progress toward writing goals for an extended period, and they have not articulated the reasons for the lack of progress, a professor can prompt, "Explain why you have not made much progress toward writing." The idea is to ensure that students continue to provide level 3 verbalizations by having them directly consider reasons for why progress is not being made.

A critical component of level 3 concurrent verbalization is allowing students to self-discover the assets or deficits of their problem-solving decisions. Thus, professors must be careful not to prompt students toward or away from any particular solution or strategy. Explicit prompts would usurp the students' independence and provide problem-solving directions that they need to develop on their own. Therefore, good or bad problem-solving moves need to be treated neutrally. While a student is engaged in a problem-solving move, the professor can probe, "Why did you write that?" or "What reason do you have for planning that?" Only after students have selected, used, and settled on a particularly good or bad strategy, procedure, or written text should a professor probe, "How do you know that this is an effective way to write?" or "Why do you think that is an effective paragraph?"

As a student draws to the end of a writing task, the professor can also ask, "Why are you almost at the end of your writing task?" or "Does your writing satisfy all the requirements for persuasion?" or "Do you need to consider anything else?" As a final step in the verbalization process, the professor could ask a level 1 prospective probe, "Now that you are finished writing, how well do you think your essay will persuade someone?" Based on students' response to this probe, professors might encourage students to engage in further revising and editing.

Instructing Students in Groups. Probing that encourages level 3 concurrent verbalization requires close monitoring of students' problem-solving behavior, and professors must be creative and flexible to generate probes as students progress. All of this is time-consuming, and professors may not have time on their side. Therefore, using level 3 concurrent verbalization in a group context may be desirable.

Mathews and others (1989) developed a "teach-aloud" technique in which participants received instruction to perform a task and then were asked to instruct the task to a partner. The participants were told to be as complete and specific as possible in describing how they were making their choices to perform the task. Results showed that participants who learned the teach-aloud technique realized greater gains in performance than participants in a control group. Professors could easily adopt a similar procedure in which they instruct specific problem-solving skills to the entire class and then break the class into dyads, with students in each dyad taking turns using level 3 concurrent verbalization to explain how they are using the new skills. The feedback that students provide to one another could further aid in the refinement and modification of their skills.

Flower (1994) has developed process-tracking observation techniques in which groups of students are encouraged to engage in metacognitive processing during problem solving by using level 3 concurrent verbalizations. The goal of these techniques is for students to examine their thoughts as they occur in response to a problem. This goal is accomplished by having students obtain independent observational records of their level 3 concurrent reports as they are engaged in problem solving. The students then examine the records with the assistance of other students.

As an illustration, consider once again the example of writing a persuasive essay. A videotape or audiotape recording of each student verbalizing as he or she is engaged in the process of planning and writing a persuasive essay is first obtained. The recording is then played back to the student and professor so that the student can observe his or her actions in carrying out the task and hear how he or she performed the writing task. With constructive feedback from the professor, the self-observations can help students balance the actual evidence of their performance against their assumptions, knowledge, and performance of the writing task (Flower, 1994). If professors have created a safe environment in the classroom, the entire class can be incorporated into the review of the student recordings for a collaborative review of each student's performance.

Caveats and Conclusion

Before engaging students in level 3 concurrent verbalizations, professors should consider two caveats to maximize their positive effects. First, metacognitive probing may be effective only when students have acquired a sufficient amount of knowledge in the content area in which the problem solving is to occur. If students are only just beginning to acquire knowledge in a domain, they may not possess the necessary concepts or procedures for explaining their problem solving.

Second, professors must consider the difficulty of the tasks that students are to perform. Problem solving, verbally encoding the problem, and verbalizing ongoing mental activity can place overwhelming demands on a student. And when excessive demands are placed on memory, students' thinking may falter, which slows their progress toward the goal. A good indication that the task is too difficult occurs when a student becomes quiet for excessively long periods or requires numerous reminders to continue talking.

We began this chapter with a cautionary remark that metacognition is not a panacea for improving students' problem solving. Metacognition comprises many components, and not every kind of metacognitive strategy will benefit students all the time. Even so, depending on students' current stage of problem solving, any one of the verbal reports discussed above may involve some aspect of metacognition that positively influences problem solving. Most important, when students seek to improve their problem-solving skills, they should not be instructed to merely use "metacognition" but instead should be directed toward specific, higher-level analyses in which they explain how they are solving the problem. These level 3 concurrent verbalizations have shown the most impressive gains in the research on learning and hold the most promise for helping students enhance their skills at problem solving.

References

Dominowski, R. L. "Verbalization and Problem Solving." In D. J. Hacker, J. Dunlosky, and A. C. Graesser (eds.), *Metacognition in Educational Theory and Practice.* Mahwah, N.J.: Erlbaum, 1998, pp. 25–46.

Ericsson, K. A., and Simon, H. A. "Verbal Reports as Data." *Psychological Review,* 1980, *87,* 215–251.

Ericsson, K. A., and Simon, H. A. *Protocol Analysis: Verbal Reports as Data.* (rev. ed.) Cambridge, Mass.: MIT Press, 1993.

Flower, L. "Metacognition: A Strategic Response to Thinking." In L. Flower (ed.), *The Construction of Negotiated Meaning.* Carbondale: Southern Illinois University Press, 1994, pp. 223–262.

Hacker, D. J. "Metacognition: Definitions and Empirical Foundations." In D. J. Hacker, J. Dunlosky, and A. C. Graesser (eds.), *Metacognition in Educational Theory and Practice.* Mahwah, N.J.: Erlbaum, 1998, pp. 1–24.

Kozulin, A. *Psychological Tools: A Sociocultural Approach to Education.* Cambridge, Mass.: Harvard University Press, 1998.

Mathews, R. C., and others. "Role of Implicit and Explicit Processes in Learning from Examples: A Synergistic Effect." *Journal of Experimental Psychology: Learning, Memory, and Cognition,* 1989, *15,* 1083–1100.

Nisbett, R. E., and Wilson, T. D. "Telling More Than We Can Know: Verbal Reports on Mental Processes." *Psychological Review,* 1977, *84,* 231–259.

DOUGLAS J. HACKER *is associate professor in the department of educational psychology at the University of Utah.*

JOHN DUNLOSKY *is associate professor in the psychology department at the University of North Carolina at Greensboro.*

11

Professors can use rubrics as a valuable evaluation tool with problem-based learning activities. In this article, we guide professors through the process of rubric development.

Assessing Students' Problem-Solving Assignments

Rebecca S. Anderson, Jane B. Puckett

In traditional classrooms, professors often assess students based on the students' abilities to recall information or comprehend simple relationships among ideas. Therefore, professors can determine students' success through multiple-choice, matching, and true-and-false tests. But in a classroom based on problem solving, students are engaged in activities that extend far beyond recalling information and understanding simple relationships. Instead, students are engaged in collaboratively analyzing, researching, and solving ill-structured problems. Students even may be engaged in developing a variety of answers to a single problem. Traditional, objective tests are not a useful tool for measuring students' success with these more complex and open-ended activities (Anderson, 1998; Darling-Hammond and Snyder, 2000). How, then, can professors in a problem-based classroom assess their students? One way is through the use of rubrics.

We begin by defining rubrics and providing examples of rubrics that we have used to assess our students. Next we offer questions that can guide readers in developing their own rubrics.

Classroom Examples of Problem-Solving Rubrics

Rubrics are evaluation tools that delineate criteria with corresponding rating scales. Rubrics clarify what is important to assess, and this clarity contributes to making problem-solving assignments as objective as possible (Moskal, 2000).

As literacy educators, we structure our classes to include numerous problem-solving tasks. For many of these tasks, we have developed a rubric

NEW DIRECTIONS FOR TEACHING AND LEARNING, no. 95, Fall 2003 © Wiley Periodicals, Inc.

for assessing students' efforts. In this section, we present example rubrics for the following activities: writing assignments, group projects, online discussions, classroom presentations, and portfolios.

Writing Assignments. Exhibit 11.1 shows an example of a writing rubric. Criteria for writing rubrics vary according to the assignment. For instance, in Exhibit 11.1, the first criterion suggests to students the importance of grounding their ideas in the academic literature, which is a criterion indicative of a research paper assignment. In another type of writing assignment—for example, a personal essay or a business letter—references to the literature would be pointless.

Notice that the rubric shown in Exhibit 11.1 (and many of the other rubrics in this article) provides the opportunity for evaluating self, peers, and teacher. In addition, Exhibit 11.1 includes space for narrative feedback. In this space, classmates and the professor can make suggestions for improvement and note areas of excellence.

Group Projects. In all disciplines, professors might find it tricky to evaluate students' efforts in group projects. Professors may not be privy to each group member's contribution. To address this issue, we administer a rubric in which students rate their own performance and the performance of each team member. This rubric is shown in Exhibit 11.2.

For each student, we average the rubrics to arrive at a rubric score. For example, if a student is in a group of four, then that student will have four rubrics—one self-evaluation and three peer evaluations. We simply add the total points and divide by the total number of rubrics.

Online Discussions. Across the nation, the number of online courses is growing. A discussion board is a common component of many of these courses. Discussion boards provide a forum where students can collaboratively analyze and solve problems (Anderson, Bauer, and Speck, 2002).

Exhibit 11.1. Writing Rubric
Please rate each of the following criteria according to scale:
1 = poor, 25 = excellent

Criteria	Self	Peer	Professor
Grounded in the academic literature (minimum of 4 citations)			
Comprehensively addresses the topic			
Includes description, details, and examples			
Written well (APA style, grammar, spelling, and punctuation are strong)			

Three Stars and a Wish: Please identify three great things about the paper and one suggestion for improvement.

Note: APA = American Psychological Association.

Exhibit 11.2. Rubric for Group Work

Evaluation for: _____	Rate: 1–20 points
1. Completed his/her share of work	_____
2. Attended all meetings	_____
3. Exhibited a positive attitude	_____
4. Contributed quality suggestions and input	_____
5. Worked effectively as a team member	_____

Professors can use a rubric weekly or several times during the semester to provide students with feedback about their online contributions. Several rubrics for this purpose already exist in the literature (see, for example, Bauer and Anderson, 2000). In Exhibit 11.3, we provide an additional example of a rubric for evaluating online discussion.

Classroom Presentations. Exhibit 11.4 shows an example of a rubric that we have used to evaluate individual and small-group presentations. Similar to our writing rubric, this presentation rubric includes space for evaluators to provide narrative comments in addition to numerical ratings.

We have found an additional advantage of using rubrics for evaluating classroom presentations. In our courses, students and instructors, as well as the students who are making the presentation, complete the rubric at the end of each presentation. Thus, student presenters receive immediate feedback from the professor and classmates who serve as the audience for the presentations.

Portfolios. Portfolios are assessment tools that have been prominent in the art world for many years. More recently, professors in a variety of disciplines have required students to create portfolios. Portfolios also are growing in popularity as an admission tool into graduate programs and as support documents during job interviews. As more students become skilled in Web design, many portfolios are no longer presented in hard form. Instead, they are presented as an electronic document shared via the Internet and commonly known as an "e-folio" (Bauer and Anderson, 2000).

Exhibit 11.3. Rubric for Online Discussion

9–10	Demonstrates an excellent understanding of key concepts; contributes in a timely and relevant manner; meets or exceeds minimum number of assigned postings; writes clearly and logically
7–8	Demonstrates an adequate understanding of most key concepts; generally contributes in a timely and relevant manner; meets minimum number of assigned postings; generally writes clearly and logically
5–6	Demonstrates a limited understanding of key concepts; contributes in a spotty manner; short perfunctory postings; writing is limited and disjointed
1–4	Rarely participates freely; short, irrelevant remarks

Exhibit 11.4. Classroom Presentation Rubric

Please rate each of the following criteria
(5 = excellent, 4 = strong, 3 = adequate, 2 = limited,
1 = seriously flawed).

Criteria	Self	Peer	Professor
Audience was actively engaged			
Presenters provided a rationale for their presentation			
Presentation was well organized			
Presenters provided handouts to support the presentation			
Overall quality of the presentation			

What was the most valuable aspect of this presentation?

_____

What would you suggest to improve this presentation?

_____

Additional comments:

_____

When students engage in problem-solving activities such as working in groups, critiquing professional literature, or completing field experiences, they create multiple products that might be worthy of inclusion in their portfolio. More important than simply presenting samples of their work, students must provide reflective explanations of what they learned while creating the products that they present. Through these reflective explanations, we gain insights into the ways students think about their own work. In fact, notice that our portfolio rubric presented in Exhibit 11.5 focuses more on assessing students' reflections than on assessing the products included in the portfolio.

Exhibit 11.5. Portfolio Rubric

Name of person submitting portfolio: _____

Evaluated by self: _____   peer: _____   instructor: _____

9–10 Well-organized, thoughtful reflections, visually attractive, strong evidence of student learning, comprehensive, excellent effort

7–8   Adequate organization, adequate reflections, somewhat attractive, some evidence of student learning, generally all areas included, adequate effort

5–6   Lacks organization, limited reflections, lacks creativity in presentation, limited evidence of student learning, all areas not included, a limited effort

1–4   A poor effort to meet any of the requirements, seriously flawed

Guiding Questions for Rubric Development

Now that we have provided examples of rubrics that we have used in our courses, we wish that we could simply develop rubrics for each of our readers' courses. Because that is not practical, we offer guiding questions that might help professors develop their own rubrics.

What Criteria Should Professors Include in Their Rubric? We hope that our examples help readers see that a good rubric carefully delineates criteria that define a "good" product. For example, in our online discussion rubric, we refer to a "minimum number of assigned postings." In other words, we find value in a certain quantity of discussion contributions, so our rubric references quantity. In our classroom presentation rubric, we refer to the need for the audience to be "actively engaged." By including this criterion in our rubric, we are helping students see our definition of a good presentation. As professors develop their own rubrics, they must determine the criteria that should be included.

Which Type of Rubric Should Professors Develop? Once professors determine the criteria for inclusion in their rubric, they must decide whether they will create a holistic or an analytical rubric (Moskal, 2000). They must decide whether they want to take a look at the students' work from a holistic perspective and score it in its entirety. Exhibit 11.5 shows an example of a holistic rubric. Holistic rubrics are advantageous when professors want to assess students' work based on the dominant impressions that the work communicates. Or, for professors who want to use an analytical rubric and score each criterion separately, Exhibit 11.4 provides an example of an analytical rubric. Analytical rubrics allow professors to evaluate students based on a more discrete consideration of each criterion.

Should a Rubric Be Designed to Allow the Opportunity for Narrative Comments? Some rubrics allow only the inclusion of quantitative markings; see Exhibit 11.5 for an example. But all rubrics can be designed to allow evaluators to write narrative feedback. See, for example, the open-ended questions in Exhibit 11.4. Professors must decide whether narrative comments are appropriate in their rubric.

We find that students are appreciative of narrative comments. Through narrative feedback, they gain stronger insights into the quality of their work. Similarly, a student's self-assessment narrative can communicate additional information to professors about that student's intent.

Will Complete Rubrics Be Handed Down at the Start of the Semester, or Will Students Be Allowed to Have Input in Rubric Development as the Semester Progresses? There are advantages to distributing and discussing course rubrics at the beginning of a semester when professors preview their syllabus. When professors distribute rubrics during the first class, students become aware at the beginning of the course what professors expect of them.

On the other hand, students benefit from having a voice in the assessment process. It is time-consuming, though, for students to participate in the total rubric development. To speed up this process, we often provide students with drafts of previously used rubrics, but then we engage them in processes that allow them to renegotiate and customize the rubrics.

Will There Be a Trial Run of the Assignment and the Application of the Rubrics? In some cases, students need to engage in the problem-solving task before negotiating the rubric criteria. For instance, most students have written research papers; therefore, they already know what constitutes a good research paper, and they can easily identify relevant criteria for evaluating research papers. On the other hand, fewer students have participated in online discussion, so until they have experience with online discussion, they may not know how to identify criteria for this task. Thus, professors might ask students to participate in online discussion before developing a rubric.

Even once students understand the criteria for a successful product and have developed a rubric, they may not know how to apply the rubric. It is important to model how to use a rubric before students are expected to complete one. One way to accomplish this is to provide an example of an assignment and lead the class through the process of evaluating the product based on the corresponding rubric.

Who Will Complete the Rubrics, and When Will They Complete Them? Professors often assume that assessment is only their responsibility. But responsibilities for assessing students can be distributed among a class through self-assessments, peer assessments, and professor-centered assessments (Knowlton and Knowlton, 2001). If professors agree that students can benefit from self-assessment and peer assessment, they should design the rubric with these different assessors in mind. For example, the rubric form should provide space for all three responses.

Inherent to this issue of self, peer, and professor-centered assessments is the timeline of when products will be assessed. For example, if students are engaged in online discussion throughout a semester, will professors complete the rubric only at the end of the semester? Perhaps the rubric could become a self-assessment and peer assessment at the midpoint of the semester. The advantage of a mid-semester evaluation based on self-assessment and peer assessment is that students have a basis for improving their work before being graded, which would occur when the professor applies the rubric at the end of the semester.

Advantages of Rubrics in Problem-Solving Environments

From this article, we hope that readers see that rubrics are flexible enough to accommodate a variety of problem-solving processes. The process of designing rubrics is flexible. Professors can design their own rubrics, or they can engage students in rubric design. Because rubrics are becoming commonplace in higher education (Anderson and Speck, 1998), professors can even adapt rubrics from other sources. A helpful Web site related to designing rubrics is http://school.discovery.com/schrockguide/assess.html.

A well-designed rubric can offer more than an assessment of "right" and "wrong" answers; instead, rubrics can help students be thoughtful about the quality of their work, which can further their own learning (Anderson, 1998). Even when professors must ultimately assign grades, the flexibility of applying rubrics broadens the possibility that a student will receive a fair grade. In our courses, for example, we determine students' final grades through a composite of rubric scores, whether a peer, the professor, or the student who created the assignment completed the rubric.

References

Anderson, R. S. "Why Talk About Different Ways to Grade? The Shift from Traditional Assessment to Alternative Assessment." In R. S. Anderson and B. W. Speck (eds.), *Changing the Way We Grade Students' Performance: Classroom Assessment and the New Learning Paradigm.* New Directions for Teaching and Learning, no. 74. San Francisco: Jossey-Bass, 1998, pp. 5–16.

Anderson, R. S., Bauer, J. F., and Speck, B. W. (eds.). *Assessment Strategies for the On-Line Class: From Theory to Practice.* New Directions for Teaching and Learning, no. 91. San Francisco: Jossey-Bass, 2002.

Anderson, R. S., and Speck, B. W. (eds.). *Changing the Way We Grade Students' Performance: Classroom Assessment and the New Learning Paradigm.* New Directions for Teaching and Learning, no. 74. San Francisco: Jossey-Bass, 1998.

Bauer, J. F., and Anderson, R. S. "Evaluating Students' Written Performance in the Online Classroom." In R. E. Weiss, D. S. Knowlton, and B. W. Speck (eds.), *Principles of Effective Teaching in the Online Classroom.* New Directions for Teaching and Learning, no. 84. San Francisco: Jossey-Bass, 2000, pp. 65–72.

Darling-Hammond, L., and Synder, J. "Authentic Assessment of Teaching in Context." *Teaching and Teacher Education,* 2000, *16,* 523–545.

Knowlton, D. S., and Knowlton, H. M. "Evaluating Students' Writing: Contextual Tensions and Practical Resolutions." *Journal for the Art of Teaching,* 2001, *8*(1), 81–91.

Moskal, B. M. "Scoring Rubrics: What, When, and How?" *Practical Assessment, Research, and Evaluation, 7,* 2000. [http://www.ericae.net/pare/getvn.asp?v=7&n=3].

REBECCA S. ANDERSON is associate professor in the department of instruction and curriculum leadership at the University of Memphis.

JANE B. PUCKETT is a doctoral student in the department of instruction and curriculum leadership at the University of Memphis.

INDEX

Back Issue/Subscription Order Form

Copy or detach and send to:

Jossey-Bass, A Wiley Company, 989 Market Street, San Francisco CA 94103-1741

Call or fax toll-free: Phone 888-378-2537 6:30AM – 3PM PST; Fax 888-481-2665

Back Issues: Please send me the following issues at $27 each
(Important: please include ISBN number with your order.)

_____

_____

_____

$ _____   Total for single issues

$ _____   SHIPPING CHARGES: SURFACE   Domestic Canadian

		Domestic	Canadian
	First Item	$5.00	$6.00
	Each Add'l Item	$3.00	$1.50

For next-day and second-day delivery rates, call the number listed above.

Subscriptions   Please __ start __ renew my subscription to *New Directions for Teaching and Learning* for the year 2__at the following rate:

U.S.	__ Individual $70	__ Institutional $145
Canada	__ Individual $70	__ Institutional $185
All Others	__ Individual $94	__ Institutional $219
Online Subscription		__ Institutional $145

**For more information about online subscriptions visit
www.interscience.wiley.com**

$ _____   Total single issues and subscriptions (Add appropriate sales tax for your state for single issue orders. No sales tax for U.S. subscriptions. Canadian residents, add GST for subscriptions and single issues.)

__Payment enclosed (U.S. check or money order only)

__VISA __ MC __ AmEx __ #_____ Exp. Date _____

Signature _____ Day Phone _____

__ Bill Me (U.S. institutional orders only. Purchase order required.)

Purchase order # _____

Federal Tax ID13559302   **GST 89102 8052**

Name _____

Address _____

_____

Phone _____ E-mail _____

For more information about Jossey-Bass, visit our Web site at www.josseybass.com

PROMOTION CODE ND03

NEW DIRECTIONS FOR TEACHING AND LEARNING IS NOW AVAILABLE ONLINE AT WILEY INTERSCIENCE

What is Wiley InterScience?

Wiley InterScience is the dynamic online content service from John Wiley & Sons delivering the full text of over 300 leading scientific, technical, medical, and professional journals, plus major reference works, the acclaimed Current Protocols laboratory manuals, and even the full text of select Wiley print books online.

What are some special features of Wiley InterScience?

Wiley Interscience Alerts is a service that delivers table of contents via e-mail for any journal available on Wiley InterScience as soon as a new issue is published online.

EarlyView is Wiley's exclusive service presenting individual articles online as soon as they are ready, even before the release of the compiled print issue. These articles are complete, peer-reviewed, and citable.

CrossRef is the innovative multi-publisher reference linking system enabling readers to move seamlessly from a reference in a journal article to the cited publication, typically located on a different server and published by a different publisher.

How can I access Wiley InterScience?

Visit http://www.interscience.wiley.com.

Guest Users can browse Wiley InterScience for unrestricted access to journal tables of contents and article abstracts, or use the powerful search engine.

Registered Users are provided with a *Personal Home Page* to store and manage customized alerts, searches, and links to favorite journals and articles. Additionally, Registered Users can view free online sample issues and preview selected material from major reference works.

Licensed Customers are entitled to access full-text journal articles in PDF, with select journals also offering full-text HTML.

How do I become an Authorized User?

Authorized Users are individuals authorized by a paying Customer to have access to the journals in Wiley InterScience. For example, a university that subscribes to Wiley journals is considered to be the Customer. Faculty, staff and students authorized by the university to have access to those journals in Wiley InterScience are Authorized Users. Users should contact their library for information on which Wiley journals they have access to in Wiley InterScience.

ASK YOUR INSTITUTION ABOUT WILEY INTERSCIENCE TODAY!

LaVergne, TN USA
26 January 2011
214099LV00001B/286/A